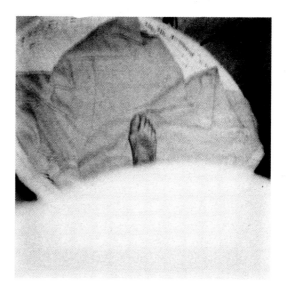

Simone Forti

Handbook in Motion

Distributed by

Contact Editions
Northampton, MA

Distributed by Contact Editions, P.O. Box 603,
Northampton, MA 01061; (413) 586-1181

First published in 1974, second edition 1980,
by The Press of the Nova Scotia College of Art and Design, Halifax, Canada
Editor: Kasper Koenig, special editor: Emmett Williams
Co-published by New York University Press, New York, NY
Third edition: Self-published, 1998

Printed by Cummings Printing Company, Hooksett, NH

ISBN: 0-937645-05-2

Introduction

From time to time someone tells me that this little book has been helpful to them, as an intimate example of an artist finding her way. This is the third edition of *Handbook in Motion, An account of an ongoing personal discourse and its manifestations in dance.* The original invitation to make a book came in 1972 from The Press of the Nova Scotia College of Art and Design. Kasper Koenig, who was the editor, was inviting certain artists to write about their work for The Nova Scotia Series, *Source Materials of the Contemporary Arts.* He included me because of the minimalist, conceptual dance/construction pieces I had made in the early sixties. But now it was the early seventies and I was feeling quite changed. This change seemed to revolve around my experience at the Woodstock Festival and an ensuing year of immersion in psychedelic culture.

The book is about movement. About working with my teachers and my colleagues, about pieces I made and the dancing I did as it evolved through various concerns. And it explores the turning points in my creative life. The body of the narrative starts with my experience at the 1969 Woodstock Festival and the year that followed. Then on page 29 it jumps back to 1955, the very beginning of my focus on dance, and moves through the years up to the festival. At page 102 it takes another jump, picking up in 1970 with my journey back from Woodstock, back to mainstream culture and to my dancing.

Now in my early sixties I'm still dancing, traveling from my home in rural northeastern Vermont to teach and perform around the world. I'm mainly focusing on how movement and language very naturally work together in our everyday lives, in our cognition and communication. I'm improvising from that root behavior, simultaneously dancing and speaking, trying to keep it earnest, light and surprising.

Simone Forti
December 1997

*The most familiar landmark: the shadow of my buggy wheel.
Round and round it went. Never moving from my line of vision as the
lines of the squares in the sidewalk measured my rocking.*

On a little island made to look like an iceberg, the polar bear passes the hours rocking his head.

Late summer in the Sierra Nevadas, a giant fir spiralled nearly imperceptibly back and forth on its axis.

An onion that had begun to sprout was set on its side on the mouth of a bottle. As the days passed it transferred more and more of its matter from the bulb to the green part, until it had so shifted its weight that it fell off.

I saw a man in pyjamas walk up to a tree, stop, regard it, and change his posture.

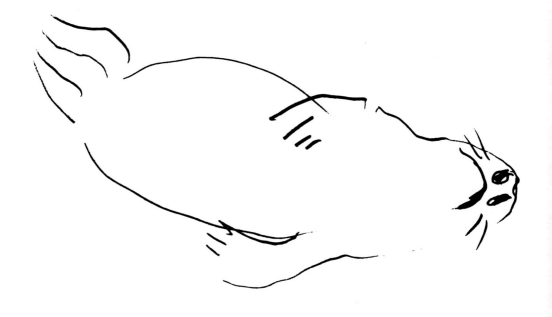

Driving along an Arizona highway, I saw a small whirlwind moving quickly along the desert. Longing to run into its center, I stopped the car and approached it on foot, but was too shy to go wildly chasing after it to catch it before it disappeared.

Father would sometimes show me historically important chess games by demonstrating them move by move on the board. I couldn't understand much about the game, but as I sat in the chair in front of the board, I felt that my body was occupying the same space, in relation to where the game was taking form, as had the body of the original player. I could feel and even smell the player. Even smell his moustache under my nose.

I held a large grasshopper in my open hand. It swayed from side to side as we gazed into each other's eyes. We sustained this alignment of sight through an exact correspondence in our movements, which created a certain resonance between us. We danced together like this for many minutes. I had just saved its life and we were very curious about each other.

The Garden

I went to the Woodstock Festival. It was the late summer of 1969. Everywhere there were people playing music together. Many were strangers to one another, many knew each other but hadn't seen one another for a long time, and everywhere there was a sense of a gathering of the tribes. I wandered around from music to music, participating where it felt natural.

There were tents everywhere, people going about their business setting up camp, comforting crying kids, playing music together, wandering. I had come with friends, and I was stoned the whole time, as we all were, half a million people stoned on hash and grass and acid for four days and nights. We all looked into one another's faces as previously I had looked only into the face of someone I was falling in love with. The kind of look that I've often wondered about, and which I associate with what psychologists call imprinting. And now we were all gazing with absolute openness, with absolute multidirectional vulnerability to imprinting, with absolute lack of fear of uniting.

I was running and dancing up and down the field, approaching different musics that I would hear more loudly as other musics faded into the distance and still others became closer. The different musics were already somewhat integrated because they were within earshot of each other. If you were in one small group you'd mainly hear your own music. But you'd also hear the music coming from down the hill, or from across a small canyon. And as I danced, my body was enough on some kind of automatic pilot that all these musics came together, somehow merged into a pattern that included them all in a dynamic, rolling kind of falling together.

You'd follow whatever interested you, regardless of day and night. And when you were tired you'd sleep. I was up in the night at one point, wandering by myself, stoned among stoned people. I wandered over to where I heard drums, and there was a fire. It was near the free stage that the Hog Farm had set up. A lot of the people were naked. Right in front of the fire a black man was moving on and on. The drums kept going, and he was doing a bouncing kind of stomping, left, right, left, right, left, right, his spine tilting from side to side. It seemed like a tuning, a finding of certain forces, an overlapping of the body into a certain bouncingness which matter can get into. Sometimes I think back on him in terms of laser light, which is so powerful not because there's so much light involved but because the light is bounced back and forth until it is tuned. As sound can become tuned. And really, it looked like after a night of doing that movement he could run a very great distance.

The hillside facing the main stage was very crowded. Many were listening to the music lying down, many were sleeping. Everyone was relaxed. To get from one place to another you had to walk right among them. No one shifted or moved to make room, you could always find a place just big enough for your foot. And you would step right down, you didn't have to nod and demonstrate that you weren't going to step on someone's hand. Everyone knew you weren't going to step on their hand. And what made it easier not to is that they wouldn't suddenly move when they saw you approaching. They'd leave their hand just as it was, you'd put your foot in the available space and go on to your next step.

It is difficult to describe the environment in which half a million people tripping together find themselves. But I perceived a set of mores regarding the sharing of space and fate which seemed to form a whole integrated way. I fell in love with that way, and remained with it for a year.

It was raining. We were looking for a place to sleep, and were told that there was a place on Ohayo Mountain. We went up there and found it. When we walked in everybody was starting to sit down on the floor to a meal. They were sitting cross-legged around a round table made out of one side of a cable spool and set on bricks. Everyone was naked. The food was on the table in large cauldrons, the bowls were stacked. It was the kind of table arrangement that could just grow and grow and include and include. There'd always be room for people to sit a little way back and make like a second circle. As new people sat down there would only be the slightest adjustment in shoulders and head tilts to include them. One thought I had at the time related to the peace conference that was going to be held in Paris. For a long time they couldn't come to an agreement on what the shape of the conference table was going to be. I remember thinking that once they did arrive at the shape of the table, one could just come in and decode it, and unravel the conclusions of the peace conference from that. A girl sort of reached towards me and silently invited me, and I stayed for three months.

We called ourselves Chia Jen, or The Family. The life we lived in common provided a matrix for the profuse visions we lived out in various twilights. Love was our totem. Associated with this was an emotional posture of continual dilation. "Flow" was central to our system, and faith in the flow of which you were a part and by which you would be sustained. And we ate no meat.

To flow was to relinquish a great deal of control over who and what you were going to come in contact or stay in contact with. You did this by suspending all plans until each moment presented itself with its many facets and its clear indications regarding your own most natural gesture. You would seldom have to interrupt a cycle of involvement because you would never have made plans to do something else. So the merging patterns could live themselves out and the whole system could integrate. One result was a very high incidence of coincidence. I came to think of coincidence as harmonic overtones of occurrence and as twilight guideposts.

There was almost a discipline of speaking only when necessary, only when the clues weren't there to be read, weren't already speaking.

You might hear the kitchen door open and shut, but you wouldn't ask who was there. You would just continue doing whatever you were doing. If for some reason you needed to know, you could find out. But most likely you didn't need to know. If you had something to tell someone, you'd wait until they needed to know. And if that time didn't come, you'd let it pass. If you were sitting near someone and you had to go to the bathroom, you wouldn't say "I'll be right back" and somehow tie them down by giving indications about what you were going to do. You'd get up and go to the bathroom. Then, if you still felt like going back, you'd go back. If they were really involved in what they were doing they'd be there when you got back. You'd sit down again, and they'd know you'd been somewhere to do something.

The spaces around us could overlap, and the silence made a great deal of that possible. And also the lack of constant judgements on each other, which perhaps had something to do with saying things only when they needed to be said. The space was sufficient for everyone because each could have the whole silence of the whole space. There wasn't the nodding and indicating that takes place when there is fear of indiscriminate union, or, more archetypally, fear of incest. Because there was no fear of incest. And we were in love with each other. We were each of us in love with nearly every one of us. And how could it be that we were in love? I don't know how it started. I came in, there it was, and I fell in love with it. I think the drugs had a lot to do with it, everybody tripping together so much. And, too, we were all gathered around Bob and Nancy, and that was how they loved.

And there were moments of terror. I never lost my sense of identity and I always knew that I was Simone. But all the acid I took seemed to break down the barriers to perception and communication between the myriad systems and processes which house the self and within which my own identity lived as one interpretation among many others with which I coexisted as in a fertile jungle of interpenetration of life. With some, in a state of symbiosis; with others, in a state of organizational competition.

Objects, though moved by people, seemed to follow their own paths, to be part of the flow. Coats would come and go, there always seemed to be one when you needed it. But if you set down a book or a tool and just wanted to leave it there for a while, you'd place it in a manner expressive of your intentions.

I always enjoyed straightening up. Each decision of what to move and just where to put it refined the discourse of how we were to live. If I was uncertain about a certain object, I would move it into an ambiguous alignment and go back the next day to find my answer.

We were not a working commune. Work found its place in our system as a natural urge to do whatever needed to be done. But since the "flow" provided for our needs, in the form of people constantly laying stuff on us, including great sacks of grains and beans, and vegetables, and dope, and even a cabin in the woods, this natural urge was never tested far beyond cooking and cleaning up.

There was an old wall or ledge of rocks outside our cabin in the woods. These rocks had long ago been piled solidly, and once it must have been a very stable wall. But through the years it had seen a lot of use and was starting to wobble. Very often, when things begin to lose their stability, slight shifts occur within them that accelerate their disintegration. I used to once in a while pass the time checking out the wall. I'd stand on it and wobble on it and check out the spots that were moving, and after a while I discovered that you had to be very much in tune with it and stand on it carefully or else it would crumble. I was involved in making a judgement about going ahead and crumbling it before somebody else might crumble it by mistake, standing on it and not being familiar with it. And one day I did see someone go down with the wall. He didn't get hurt, he kept his balance throughout. The wall crumbled under his feet and he just sort of rode it down.

Once, on mescaline, I started weaving the upper half of my body very fast in a figure-eight, supporting and compensating with my lower half. I could do it only if I got the exactly correct dynamic and rhythm going — the exact amount of thrust in one direction that I could then recoil and bring back in the other direction and just keep it weaving back and forth. I couldn't have done one side of the movement without the other side. It was like jumping onto a ride. I've often had that feeling about movement, about rides in movement that you can find with your body formations. They remind me of perpetual-motion machines. I guess twirling is the simplest one. I think of twirling as a

19

ride. A force that you can ride. So I rode the figure-eight.

I went off the pill. Two years before, I had written: "It's funny, now I've started on the pill. It's the loss of my own natural rudder. My own timing. My contact with the moon. My endocrine system that's given me my form, my cycle." I'd come to feel that I'd locked into one of my states of feeling, and remained in it. When I went off the pill my trust in our way of life became more real.

I've wondered a lot about contraception. And I've found it a mystery that, with our technology, we haven't found a better solution. One day someone said to me: "But there cannot be one." I have come to believe that the ideal contraception is self-knowledge, knowledge of one's own cycles, and a sense of the resonance between the cycles of everyone in the community.

There must have been cultures where there was a gracious balance of erotic flow, and sometimes sitting one out. Maybe you'd know that you were fertile right then, and didn't want to conceive. Or you didn't want to hurt someone's feelings, and you'd just cool it. And everyone would understand each other, not just verbally, but through sensing movements. Someone would be blooming, someone would be at high tide, and someone would be at low tide. And dancing would help it stay in a circle, help the moment of conception find its place, and there'd be a moderate crop of babies.

When cold weather came I spent days upon days watching the fire. Watching the changes, the crumblings, watching the heating that accompanies a crumbling as new surfaces are revealed, watching the coolings as a flaming log burns through and breaks in two, each half falling away from the center of heat. I remember feeling that sitting in front of the fire was equivalent to sitting in the sun. And equivalent to bathing. Or baking instead of bathing. The body smells would cook down to a kind of fresh live sweetness, and I would tune into the smell of me. In doing this I tuned into my feelings in a deeper sense. I developed a deeper understanding of my times of heat and non-heat, and, perhaps, in a much more subliminal way, mainly through reading movements, I tuned into the balance of the people around me.

We had no electricity, but we did have a small battery-operated record player. We did a lot of singing along with it, getting into a lot of

20

elaboration, so that eventually we were jamming with the records and dancing. Mainly only a few of the women were doing it, it was something that just went on. After we weren't in the cabin any longer, but in a house that was sort of spread out and all strung together, there was one room that became the women's room because, well, because the sewing machine was in there. So was the record player, and often we'd get to dancing. I remember using the term "sounding center." That room seemed like the sounding center of the house. It was the spot from which you could hear all the sounds from all parts of the house, and incorporate them all in your dancing and your singing. You'd be a kind of receiver and transmitter between the parts of the house. It happened subliminally.

A few of us played instruments, and often there'd be musicians passing through. Both music and dancing had a great power over the rhythm of the day, over the cycles of daily life. Helping us stay apart, bringing us together, precipitating tides of festivity. I had been a dancer, and one thing that struck me then was that I was still dancing. I was still making movement studies, and getting into new areas of dynamics. I was continuing to dance to music, able to stick with the rock dancing I had gotten into, to do it as much as I wanted, and to take it out of the limitations of the social situation of couple dancing. I didn't have to especially identify myself as one who danced, so I was left free to delve into dancing and to function in the ways I knew best.

For a period of time I was waking up very early, going out while others were still asleep, and dancing, working on movement, rejoicing in the morning. Sometimes a couple of people might be up, starting the oatmeal, and they'd see what I was doing. It all fit together, the dancing and the cooking.

One morning I stood on a big round rock and put a heavy rock on my head. I was willing to be still, balanced on the rock and balancing the other rock on my head, but in order to keep it together I had to keep a very slight movement, a tiny dance, going on between the two rocks. That went on for many minutes. No one else was awake.

I saw a crane fly by
So dark and so slowly
And not three paces on
A mallard drowned at sea
A chill of fear passed through
I knew that I must flee

Angel angel I'm watching over you

My bells they are my friend
At night they light my path
When snowflakes hide the moon
Their song reveals your face

Angel angel I'm watching over you

Once in the woods I lived
Together with my friends
The days rolled by like flowers
The bees they watched in awe
The spirits came to join
Our family of love

Angel angel I'm watching over you

Our Martha went to jail
We quickly raised the bail
And in our hearts were glad
That she had worn the flag

Angel angel I'm watching over you

The cabin had a barn, and on the night of the first snow the barn burned down. We were kicked out, and The Family headed north. I stayed on the road for a while, going back and forth, crashing around. I finally hooked up with Martha, one of my old Chia Jen sisters. There was a house in town where crashers were nearly always welcome. I myself had been quietly welcomed on a rainy November night. I had stayed there for two or three nights and then gone on my way. Then in mid-winter I crashed there with Martha. It worked out well for all concerned. Just then they had no women to look after the place, so we stayed. New faces kept passing through, people needing a blanket and a place by our fire. Martha and I once found a couple of young girls drunk and crying in the snow. They stayed on with us.

But the scene was changing. The lease passed from the hands of a 16-year-old freak who had been contracting jobs for the whole house, to a 25-year-old sculptor who wanted to turn the house into an art gallery. He tried to kick the young girls out. There was no reason for me to be there anymore. I felt I could no longer accept anything I wasn't free to share with anyone whose path crossed mine. So together with the other two chicks, Martha and I moved to a field with the site of a burnt-down farmhouse, a good well, and a few standing shacks. There had been a couple of summer music festivals there, which had left as their legacy some chemical toilets, making the place a likely one for transient settlements. The festivals had also left a small wooden platform of a stage weathering in the middle of the field.

When we arrived, snow was still on the ground. There, in a shack, we found a guy who'd been kicked out of our old place because people had thought he was a junky. He was simply very pale and desperately withdrawn into a tortured silent monologue about an avenging god. He was living without heat, the wind blowing through the walls. We stapled newspapers and cloth to the walls, and the sculptor from our old place got us a coal stove.

There had been two summers of communities there before us, and a few winter hermits. A foxy young fellow named Wolfe came to live with us. He carried the coal sack in from town and filled his bowl at our fire. Everywhere I found plates and pots encrusted with last summer's last soups. The last pot that had been abandoned was the easiest to find and clean and the first to be used again.

We had the fire and the well, and our goal was to establish an even cycle of meals so that even our withdrawn Hypno would get up in the morning and life would clarify into some dignity. It was a matter of washing a couple of buckets in the icy stream, getting water from the well across the field, chopping wood until the coal came, and getting the dishes going, and the beans. Where were the beans to come from? I brought in a few beans and carrots myself. If we could only get a center of energy going, other energies would come to it. A farmer up the road was giving us a quart or two of goat's milk every day.

There was always dope around. And there were always runaways. Cops would come around often looking for one runaway or another. They'd just stay outside and ask anyone they saw if they'd seen a fifteen-year-old blond named so-and-so. But it was our custom for no one to know anyone's last name. I'd be across the field washing clothes beside the stream and notice the cop car and calmly go about my business. We'd all just calmly go about our own business, knowing that whoever talked to the cops would have calm, positive vibes and all would go well. I felt that the spirits liked us, and were helping us.

Towards late spring three commune busses arrived. We were becoming a thriving community of about forty people. The men built brick ovens and a sauna, and rearranged the stones of our central fire back and forth to make a cooking fire in the daytime and a sitting-around fire at night. I helped some friends get started in a health-food business, and they gave us sacks of beans and oats. And the stream was full of watercress and mint.

On the first really sunny Sunday there was a picnic on the town baseball field. Everywhere were people greeting and embracing, settling into small groups, making music, wandering from group to group, and children running. I was dancing between the musics, running up and down the field, approaching these drums and then those, greeting people I hadn't seen all winter, and I was happy. From time to time I'd run over to a spot near the edge of the field where somehow the mothers of the very new babies had gathered. The Family had returned from Vermont with a new baby, and I'd take a peek at little Rhea, sleeping in the shade of an umbrella. My own period was past due, and

I was just wondering.

Booming over the various musics the loudspeakers suddenly were on with a "testing, testing," and everyone stopped playing. All the circles were polarized towards the platform, and everyone waited through a good half hour of crackling and popping and "testing, testing." Then finally a group played for us as we all listened. And they sang the news of a tragedy at Johnson's Pastures, where a barn had burned down with three of our friends inside.

I wasn't around the day the cops told us the busses had to go and the tents come down. As I heard the story, first the busses left and then the cops. I think we could have gotten away with leaving the tents up. After all, we were performing a function for the town, and the cops knew it. We were a free and orderly campground just outside of Woodstock, and people passing through were told about us. It was just a matter of keeping us down to size. But we were an anarchy, and some had taken it upon themselves to see that the cops' orders were carried out to the letter.

The night after the tents came down I was sitting by the campfire, no idea what I would do next. Everyone was heading out in different directions and it struck me that I hoped to God that I wasn't pregnant. Then Martha came up to me, and told me a story. She had been lying in the grass a few yards from the fire. She had felt like turning around, putting her feet to the uphill side, just to feel more comfortable. Two minutes later a car had driven onto the field and run over her foot. Two minutes earlier it would have been her head. Again the spirits were helping us. We were being told that it was time to leave. Our territory had lost definition to the extent that a car could drive right by our fire.

In my bag I had some keys that La Monte Young and Marian Zazeela had given me. The keys to their loft in New York. And that was our next stop.

La Monte was studying singing ragas with the Indian master, Pandit Pran Nath. He introduced me to his teacher as the Italian folksinger he'd told him about, and had me sing him a song. It was decided that I, too, should have at least a taste of studying with Pran Nath, and so I showed up for my first appointment of any kind in more than a year. I had about eight lessons, which I loved very much. Guruji, as a master is affectionately called, thought my pitch was precise "like a pin," and he advised me to go to India to study singing in an ashram, where I would lead "a very pure life." Pran Nath said the tamboura would be a sword in my hand.

I didn't know what to make of it all. I loved the singing, but my elbows were pulling in at my sides, my chin was pulling into my neck, my eyes were pulling down to the ground, and my palms were pulling together. My natural gravity directed me to Los Angeles for my periodic visit to my parents. Once there, I felt, perhaps I would know what to do.

The evening before my departure, I was standing with new-found friends in front of the Roma Cafe in Manhattan's Little Italy. A motorcycle pulled up, and a helmetted Charlotte Moorman stepped down. We exchanged greetings, and, on hearing that I was going West, she asked me if I knew that many of my old friends were there, teaching at the new California Institute of the Arts. I did not. She gave me Alison Knowles' phone number, and Allan Kaprow's.

The next day I boarded a plane for Los Angeles.

Alison was living in a big house in the Hollywood Hills. There were others living there, too, all of them related to the new art college. There was room for me there in the big house, and they wanted me among them. I could see it and feel it.

The college was offering Tai Chi, a Chinese martial art, which very much interested me. Allan arranged that I could take all the classes I wished, in exchange for substituting for him from time to time. The money my parents had given me was running out, and suddenly I realized that I had just about enough margin on which to pull myself together. I kept thinking about that sword in my hand, and I returned to dancing as a self-conscious art as to an old friend.

I met Ann Halprin in 1956. I was 21, and recently married. I had met my husband, Bob Morris, in college. We'd both quit school, and were living in San Francisco. From the very first day at Ann's workshop I knew that I wanted to study with her. It was the first time a teacher had really captured my imagination, and the first time I knew I would always do a lot of dancing. I studied and performed with Ann for four years. The main thing she taught me was how to learn from my own body intelligence.

I remember the first rudimentary improvisation problem in which I participated. We must have been a group of about fifteen people. Ann had us walk together in a circle, not single-file but simply all moving in the same direction around a general circular path. She asked us to follow the speed of the flow around the circle, and not to initiate any changes. We started out very slow, and over a period of an hour gradually picked up more and more speed until we were running. We ran for some time and then started to slow down. The slowing-down process was much faster than the speeding-up process. Within this general speeding up, running and slowing down there were several minor speed-ups and slow-downs. We finally came to a stop and collapsed on the ground.

Ann approached technique through the idea that the body is capable of doing all kinds of movement. She gave us such problems as running while moving the spine through any possible positions. We called such problems "explorations." The body would give whole responses around the point of predetermination, and would come out with movement that went beyond plan or habit. We spoke of expanding our movement vocabulary. And it did seem that the more movement one explored, the more material one could season and articulate. And of course each new kind of movement that one came upon was a welcome surprise.

Every movement, every stepping off a curb, every fall of a leaf has its own particular quality. We used the term "movement quality" to help us focus on this particularity of essence, and to help us not discriminate against any movement we could experience.

Another term we used a lot was "kinaesthetic awareness." The kinaesthetic sense has to do with sensing movement in your own body,

sensing your body's changing dynamic configurations. But it's more than that. I can remember just waking from dreams and still having a sense of the dream landscape not only in my memory but in my limbs as well.

During this time I was also teaching a course in modern dance at Dominican College in San Rafael. The first day I met with the girls I talked to them about kinaesthetic awareness. I told them that as they watched me talk they could tell a lot about what was going on in me. They could do this simply by watching how I held myself, and at exactly what instant I shifted my weight. They could sense these rhythms and tensions, they could sense how what they saw, felt. I think that if Ann gave us an aesthetic point of judgement, it was that there should be a live kinaesthetic awareness in the mover.

Ann lived in the country, and we did a lot of observing of the movement around us. Watching ants in an ant-hill, watching water, watching trees, watching people. One day A.A. Leath, a senior member of the workshop, was teaching the class. He gave us the problem of individually selecting something in the environment and observing its movement for half an hour. We were then to abstract an element from the observed movement that we could take on in our own bodies. Once in a while Bob Morris would attend A.A. Leath's classes, and I remember vividly the movement Bob did on this particular day. He had observed a rock. Then he lay down on the ground. Over a period of about three minutes he became more and more compact until the edges of him were off the ground, and just the point under his center of gravity remained on the ground.

Ann's studio was a deck, or platform, right out in the woods. I have memories of lying on the deck, then convulsing with such energy that I'd just pop up into the air and fall down again. Then, from however I'd landed, I'd convulse again and pop up and fall down again and again.

Another memory I have of those days is of a movement Trisha Brown did. She was holding a broom in her hand. She thrust it out straight ahead, without letting go of the handle. And she thrust it out with such force that the momentum carried her whole body through the air. I still have the image of that broom and Trisha right out in

31

space, traveling in a straight line about three feet off the ground.

Our basic way of working was improvisation following the stream of consciousness. We worked at achieving a state of receptivity in which the stream of consciousness could spill out unhampered. But at the same time a part of the self acted as a witness, watching for movement that was fresh and good, and watching the whole of what was evolving between us. At times, after a session, I had the feeling that even if I died that night, as one might die any night, the improvisation had grounded itself, and had become an autonomous moment of communion.

We were not interested in having ideas about how our movements should relate, but in looking at how things did relate. Sometimes there seemed to be some obvious association, or some cause-and-effect relationship. Often there was a coexistence, a juxtaposition of qualities or concerns, from which would emerge a third quality, the quality of the space between those two coexisting spaces.

Eventually we started including a lot of verbal material. Once words started appearing in our improvisations, there was a tremendous expansion in the kinds of juxtapositions we could articulate.

About that time I read Kurt Schwitters' scenario for a Merz play in which people were to be tied to backdrops as part of the structure, while a sewing machine rattled along in the lead role.

During our four years in San Francisco, Bob had been painting Abstract Expressionist works. I had expressed an interest in doing some painting, and he had encouraged me to the point of building me a palette table, and teaching me to stretch the huge canvases I needed. Sometimes I would start a painting by taking a nap on a freshly stretched canvas. I painted pretty intensely for about six months, but all the while I continued dancing with Ann and the workshop.

Meanwhile, in the night, I would often wake up startled, dancing in my sleep. One of my recurrent sleep-dances always ended in my reaching past the mattress and loudly rapping my knuckles on the floor. I think that improvisation was really beginning to pain me. I can remember saying that my inner ear could no longer take those limitless seas. There just seemed to be all this turmoil and turning of image upon image.

I find it interesting that at just this same time Abstract Expressionism seemed to stop. I've always wondered at its sudden end. Like a sudden death. Or a sudden glimpse of a precipice, and then everybody stopped. And no one talks about it. It's like a collective blind spot. Yet even to this day the sight of a de Kooning can radically change my breathing.

I began to hear about the Gutai group in Japan. A photograph of one of their pieces made a deep imprint on my mind. The picture showed a man and a group of logs. The logs were standing in the form of a cone, their tops leaning together in the center. The man stood beneath the center of the cone. In his hands he held an axe, poised ready to swing.

In the spring of 1959, Bob Morris and I moved to New York. I just couldn't believe that place. What shocked me most was being immersed in an environment that seemed to have been completely designed and created by people. It was like a maze of concrete mirrors. It was very depressing. I remember how refreshing and consoling it was to know that gravity was still gravity. I tuned into my own weight and bulk as a kind of prayer.

We found a nice little loft, and for a while I worked there, and even kept dance notes in a notebook. I'd do things like placing a stool in the middle of the room, and a roll of toilet paper over by the wall, and then sitting somewhere on the floor, and from time to time moving something. It seemed so sad to be working alone in that loft. It was so hard to keep the floor clean, it was such a silly floor. Bob had stopped painting. He was actively trying to do nothing, but actually he was reading voraciously.

I started going to classes at the Martha Graham school, but I could not hold my stomach in. I *would not* hold my stomach in. Then I started going to the Merce Cunningham school. I remember watching my teachers, and feeling that I couldn't even perceive what they were doing, let alone do it. A teacher would demonstrate a movement, I'd see only this flashing blur of feet, and I wouldn't know what had happened. I just couldn't do it. An important element of the movement seemed to be the arbitrary isolation of the different parts of the body. I recall a statement I made in exasperation one day in the studio. I said that Merce Cunningham was a master of adult, isolated articulation. And that the thing I had to offer was still very close to the holistic and generalized response of infants.

I took a job in a nursery school. On rainy mornings we'd take the children to a big empty room in the basement to play. There was one boy who always spent some of that time going over and over a particular movement he had invented and obviously found very satisfying. He would roll a ball, and then, running past it, fling himself onto his stomach, sliding on, and pivoting as he slid, so that as his momentum slowed to a stop, he would arrive in position just in time for the ball to roll into his outstretched arms.

I listened a lot to the music of La Monte Young. He was working with sustained tones: sound that had a lot of distinguishable parts within it, yet the parts were present all at once, and the sound didn't change very much in the course of its duration. The music had a sense of natural, untampered existence, and I was grateful to hear it.

The first work I came across in New York that I felt an immediate kinship with was a piece by Bob Whitman called "E.G." Part way through it, Whitman took a flying leap directly over the heads of the audience. It looked like he was going to come crashing down into the crowd when, just in the nick of time, he grabbed some bars which he had installed in the ceiling, and swung away out of sight. In the background a tape played, barely audible. You could just make out things like "yes yes yes . . . munch munch munch . . ." It was hard to take in everything because the room was crowded. But I was very moved by the event.

After it was over, I went into the back room and told Whitman that I'd been doing things in California which I felt were similar to his piece, and that I would like to work with him. He looked very sceptical, but he did take my phone number. And several months later he invited me to participate in "The American Moon."

During the performance my tasks mostly involved working the apparatus of the environment — climbing the ladder, stomping around on and rattling the rather precarious scaffolding, reaching to switch lights off and on, covering another performer with rags, crawling under an inflating balloon. Only seldom did I appear as a figure. In one image I rolled on the ground over another figure rolling towards me, like two logs might roll across each other, and then disappeared. It struck me that most of my actions were done not in order that the movement be seen, but so that the particular task could be accomplished. And it struck me too that the movement had its own presence.

The one teacher I connected with in New York was Bob Dunn. He was teaching a composition class at the Merce Cunningham studio in the fall of 1960. Dunn began the course by introducing us to John Cage's scores. One score, "Imperfections Overlay", involved pages of clear plastic on which there were dots that corresponded to the imperfections Cage had found in some sheets of paper. These pages of clear plastic were to be dropped onto a graph. Where the dots fell determined when and where the events were to be performed. But the nature of the events to be performed in those time and spatial relationships was left completely up to the choice of the performer. Such an event could be the sound of a bell, it could be falling off a cliff, it could be anything. It did not seem to me that Cage had relinquished any control, but rather that he had shifted his hand to a new dimension or point of leverage. His hand could still be strongly felt in the original structuring of the procedure, and in the resulting quality of space containing autonomous events.

In retrospect, I find that "Imperfections Overlay", with its graph, was my first exposure to a still point of reference that gives a footing for a precise relationship to indeterminate systems. I had the feeling that the resultant piece would be a kind of ghost or trace of all the elements involved, including the original sheets of paper, and the air currents through which the plastic sheets had glided. It seemed to be a kind of notation whose interpretation by the performer would reawaken a partial presence of the original events.

The Cage scores got the class off to a good start. They provided us with a clear point of departure, and performing them had the effect of helping us bypass inhibitions on making pieces. We started producing a lot of material, and, once we were rolling, we had something to learn from. Especially towards the beginning of the course, Dunn urged us to work on our own pieces quickly, without suffering over them. And throughout the course he urged us to be clearly aware of the methods we were using in working, whatever they might be. This meant being clear about the conception of any piece. Implied within the first conception was also the process that was going to lead from it to the final performance. Realizing that one could choose the distance between the point of control and the final movement performed, I came to see control as being a matter of placement of an effective act within the interplay of many forces, and of the selection of effective vantage points. This made me start trying to take precise readings of what points of control I was using, and wanted to use, and to what effect.

That Christmas, Robert Whitman invited me to participate in a group evening at the Reuben Gallery. I did "Rollers" and "See-Saw".

BULK RATE
U. S. Postage
PAID
New York, N. Y.
Permit No. 11023

REUBEN GALLERY
44 East 3rd Street
New York 3, N. Y.

happenings AT THE Reuben Gallery

THE REUBEN GALLERY PRESENTS ITS CHRISTMAS PROGRAM OF HAPPENINGS:

"V A R I E T I E S" December 16, 17, 18 at 8:30 p.m.

A SHINING BED	by	Jim Dine
SEE SAW	by	Simone Morris
CHIMNEYFIRE	by	Claes Oldenburg
ERASERS	by	Claes Oldenburg

All patrons are urged to reserve their seats in advance by sending in their tax-deductible contributions, now. Admission cannot be guaranteed unless reservations are made. Contribution: $1.50.

Capacity - 50. Admission by advance reservation -- please make your reservations by mail.

RESERVATION COUPON
(Please make checks payable to the) Reuben Gallery, 44 East 3rd. Street, N.Y.C. 3, N.Y.

I enclose $_____, my contribution to NEW HAPPENINGS AT THE REUBEN GALLERY.
Please hold reservations in my name for _____(no. of seats) for _____(date).

NAME: _____

ADDRESS: _____

two short pieces by Claes Oldenburg.

A SHINING BED
BY JIM DINE

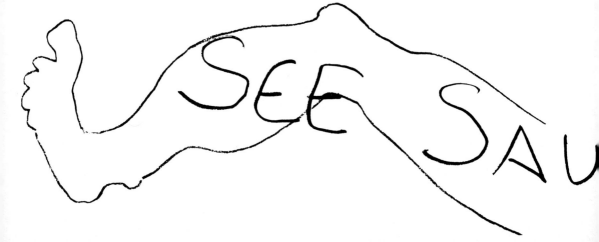

SEE SAU

SEE-SAW

This piece, performed by a man and a woman, is about twenty minutes long. It requires a plank about eight feet long, and a saw-horse, used together as a see-saw. At each end of the plank, three hooks correspond to hooks placed in the two opposite walls. Elastics are attached from the hooks in the walls to the hooks in the boards, forming a long line from wall to wall which zigs and zags as the see-saw shifts balance back and forth. Attached to the bottom of one side of the see-saw is a noise-making toy that goes "moo" every time it is tipped.

The beginning of "See-Saw" was signaled by the lights going off and on at intervals of about six seconds. The man, Bob Morris, appeared in a black coat, carrying the saw-horse, went back for the plank, and set up the see-saw. He attached the elastics and hooked up the "moo" toy. He pushed the see-saw up and down a few times, and each time the toy went "moo". The woman, Yvonne Rainer, also appeared wearing a black coat. Both took off their coats, revealing red sweaters and shorts. All this time the lights had been going off and on, and stayed on only after the two had climbed onto the see-saw.

For a long time they simply see-sawed up and down. Then they did several combinations of movements which shifted the balance. The possibilities are endless, for the whole structure of plank and performers rests on one point, making its equilibrium as sensitive as a pair of scales. Any change in the arrangement of body parts, the slightest change of position by either performer, affects the balance of the entire setup. Holding the see-saw level, or controlling the degree of tilt in either direction, requires a coordination by the two performers of actions of compensating effect on the equilibrium.

A section followed in which Yvonne tossed and turned, throwing herself around and shrieking as she rode the see-saw up and down. Again, during this section, the lights were going off and on. Bob pulled a copy of Art News out of his pocket and read aloud in a monotonous, self-contained voice. Towards the end the lights stayed on, and Bob and Yvonne stood side by side in the center of the board, their arms around each other's shoulder. They balanced the board by shifting

their knees, causing it to balance gently back and forth.

From where I had been working the lights I sang this song, a song I had once heard on a record:

Way out on a sun-baked desert
Where nature favors no man
A buffalo met his brother
At rest on the sun-baked sand.

The buffalo said to his brother
What ailment got you this way
But his brother never said
Cause his brother was dead
Been dead since way last May.

Way out on a sun-baked desert
I heard a big Indian moan
So I left my tent
Cause I knew what it meant
I swore I'd never more roam.

Was evening when I stopped running
My legs was tired and sore
I lost fifty pounds
On the desert grounds
I knew I'd lose fifty more.

Finally, Bob tipped his side down, the toy went "moo" for the last time, and they walked down the board.

ROLLERS

"Rollers" requires two wooden boxes approximately one foot and a half wide, two and a half feet long, and one foot deep. These are open at the top and set on swivel wheels. Each box has a hole drilled towards the top of each of three of its sides, with a rope approximately six feet long fastened to each hole. Two performers, each sitting in one of the boxes, improvise a duet of vocal sounds while six members of the audience pull on the ropes, giving the singers a ride. The three ropes fastened to the boxes seem to create a situation of instability, and in no time the boxes are careening wildly. For the singers in the boxes, this produces an excitement bordering on fear, which automatically becomes an element in their performance.

Mar 13

I guess at different times I'll
be writing about different things
& in different ways.
  #1 I can't decide ~~to~~ to
plunge into dance effort.
  #2 I can't decide to just
stop all-together.
  I'd love to go on a long
cross country trek. Ah
fresh air. But I know I'll
half drag along with this
art business for some time
to come.

play made permanent.
Teaching nursery school one
can't be so narrow as
to hold one style of
reasoning above another
in or de-ductive, improvised
or planned. All are used
sometimes one,
sometimes another

I do have an idea for a sculpture
but if I make it then what will
I do with it, I would hate to
have it. Here it is:

It might even be fun to make.
But what then? What then? Got
a letter from Aunt H. Seems
things are jumping there.
And yet . . . . . I don't want
to be jumping. Waiting
Waiting to see?

children but I can't manage
the externals of the teacher role.
I can't seem to take on the
ear-marks of the bourgeois adult.
They think I'm childish. No. It's
not childishness. It's just an
other way of being. If I were
fifty I couldn't do like they
do. No it's not childishness.
It's an other way of being. Not
a better way, but they seem
threatened.
Mar 29
    art — formaldehide
know I'm aclimated to N.Y. And
because I'm sick of everything.
pickey-headed professional young women.
art beaurocracy — possible to work
outside of. One must not expect anyones
respect. Might even lose friendships.
    Losing taste for "center". Everything
else equally disgusting.

April 27 Sick in bed. Haven't been wanting to write. How are things? No convictions. And yet I go on. Thinking about : art. Why? Maybe for the same reasons that I'm not somewhere in the Amazon this minute. Just the continuing set up of my life. Art isn't a physical interest for me any more like it was when I was dancing. It's just a role which more or less continues. Yes I'll be doing a loft concert. That does interest me. The responsability part of it interests me. Maybe in Sept I'd like to start teaching. To organize a group, in the

form of a class to bring
together kinaesthetic movement intelligence with
a real use of ideas in
the form of props or
organizational formal
ideas.

I prefer to see _something_
rather many things in
composition. If there is
composition at all I prefer
to see something happen,
some radical change
take place in the course of
the "piece" rather than
to see many varied
shiftings. If there are many
varied shiftings I prefer

that they be hap-hazard
like the shiftings of
scean and attention
during a walk.

May 1

Feeling low. Mabe it's because
spring is so late in starting.
It's so damp and oh ?
Don't much like our new
place. It's big, but I don't
like it's bigness. It seems
more closed off. I miss the
the court-yard space. I
miss the noise, the people
in their windows. This place
is closed off and damp. I've
gotten so far away from
dance. In all ways. So
completely. And yet I still
respond. To what? Oh
This concert I'm doing is very

thin. And yet it must show
up something. It must be
the vehicle for something
some attitude some form
which I just take for granted
and which is a particle of
value. And maybe not. I'm
ashamed to dance. I can't
stand this anal dance
movement they teach in technique classes and yet I'm
ashamed to move with respons.
Ashamed? Well I just can't
do it any more. If I just
stretch I could almost bash
my teeth out.
May 2. Feeling very low tonight.

In the spring of 1961, La Monte Young asked me to do an evening in a series that was taking place in a loft on Chambers Street. I can still remember sitting on the bed one afternoon with a pad of paper and crayons on my lap, drawing up the dance constructions. I called the evening "five dance constructions and some other things". I think of it as the pilot concert for the work I was to do for years to come. I have no photographs from that concert, but I've done nearly all of those pieces again, and the pictures that follow were taken at later concerts. The pieces come in the sequence in which they were originally shown.

SLANT BOARD

"Slant Board" is a dance construction. It requires a wooden ramp eight feet square leaned against a wall so that it forms a surface inclined at about a 45-degree angle to the floor. Along the top of the inclined plane five or six holes are drilled and a rope fastened into each. The ropes are knotted at approximately one-foot intervals, and when not in use reach almost to the bottom of the board. The piece begins when three or possibly four people get on the ramp. They have been instructed to keep moving from top to bottom and from side to side of the board, which can be done only by using the ropes. The movement should not be hurried, but calm, and as continuous as possible. The activity of moving around on such a steep surface can be strenuous even when done casually. If a performer needs to rest he may do so by using the ropes any way he can to assume a restful position. But the performers must stay on the board for the duration of the piece. It was first performed for ten minutes, and should last long enough for the audience to walk around and observe it. I suggest the performers wear tennis shoes.

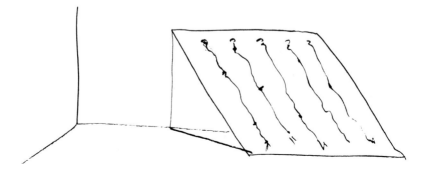

HUDDLE

Another Dance Construction

"Huddle" requires six or seven people standing very close together, facing each other. They form a huddle by bending forwards, knees a little bent, arms around each other's shoulders and waists, meshing as a strong structure. One person detaches and begins to climb up the outside of the huddle, perhaps placing a foot on someone's thigh, a hand in the crook of someone's neck, and another hand on someone's arm. He pulls himself up, calmly moves across the top of the huddle, and down the other side. He remains closely identified with the mass, resuming a place in the huddle. Immediately, someone else is climbing. It is not necessary to know who is to climb next. Everyone in the huddle knows when anyone has decided to be next. Sometimes two are climbing at once. That's O.K. And sometimes sounds of laughter come from the huddle. The duration should be adequate for the viewers to observe it, walk around it, get a feel of it in its behavior. Ten minutes is good. The piece has also been formed in such a way that, as it ended, each of the performers found six other people from the audience to get a second-generation huddle going, until six were happening simultaneously.

2nd huddle with from instructions

slant board

wall with pipes for from instructions

accompaniment

1st huddle

platforms

hangers

see saw

HANGERS

Also a Dance Construction

"Hangers" requires some preparation. Five ropes are required, each tied to form a long loop hanging from the ceiling to within a foot of the floor. Hanging in each rope stands a person. Each of these "hangers" stands with one foot in the bottom of the loop of his rope. A small block of wood placed between the foot and the rope makes this position a lot more comfortable. It is important that each hanger center his body well between the two sides of his rope. The hangers are instructed simply to stand passively. There are four "walkers" who are instructed to walk, weaving in and out among the hangers, and among each other. The ropes should not be hung in a straight line, and should be close enough to each other that, as the walkers walk among the hangers, they can't help but gently bump them, causing them to roll and sway. When the piece was first performed it lasted five minutes, but it could last ten or for whatever time seems in proportion to the rest of the situation.

PLATFORMS

This piece is a dance construction and a duet for whistling. It requires
two platforms (wooden boxes without bottoms) and two performers,
preferably a man and a woman. The platforms should each be long
enough and high enough to hide a person, but they should not be
exactly alike. They are placed in the room some distance apart. The
man helps the woman get under her platform, walks over to his, and
gets under it. Under the platforms, the two gently whistle. They can
easily hear each other, for the boxes act as resonating chambers, making
the sound clear and penetrating. It is important that the performers
listen to each other. Their whistling should come from the easy
breathing of a relaxed state of easy communion. Each inhalation should
be silent, and as long as in normal breathing. The piece goes on for
about fifteen minutes. The man should wear a watch, so that he knows
when the designated time is up. He emerges from under his platform,
and helps the woman from under hers.

ACCOMPANIMENT FOR LA MONTE'S 2 sounds
AND LA MONTE'S 2 sounds

This piece is an accompaniment for "2 sounds", a twelve-minute tape
by La Monte Young. The tape is a recording of two continuous, very
loud and complex sounds, one of very low frequency and one of very
high, playing simultaneously. The accompaniment requires one rope and
one person to ride in the rope. The rope ends are tied together to form a
long loop, which is fastened to the ceiling, and hangs to within a foot
of the floor. The rope should be discretely positioned in the room so
that it can be viewed casually, its off-center location clearly indicating
that it is an accompaniment to the principal event, La Monte's tape.
The piece begins when a person gets into the rope. A second person
turns on the tape, slowly turns the person in the rope round and round
and round until the rope is completely wound up, and walks away. The
sound fills the space. The rope unwinds, then rewinds on its own
momentum, unwinds and rewinds on and on until, finally, it becomes
still. The unwinding ends many minutes before the tape is over. The
person remains in the rope, hanging plumb and listening.

FROM INSTRUCTIONS

One man is told that he must lie on the floor during the entire piece. Another is told that he must tie the first man to the wall. The room in which the piece was first performed had pipes running along the wall. Some similar structure is required. As the men's instructions are conflicting, the result is a physical conflict. During the first performance, a short time after "From Instructions" started a second "Huddle" took place in another part of the room. Certainly everyone was aware that the huddle was going on, and looked at it from time to time, but most of the attention focused on "From Instructions".

CENSOR

One person shakes a pan full of nails very loudly, while another sings a song very loudly. The volume should be in perfect balance.

HERDING

Six people walked up to members of the audience and very casually asked, "Would you mind moving that way?" It took a while for the audience to realize that this was happening to every one of them. We herded the audience to one end of the room, then got behind them and herded them back, saying, "Would you mind going over there? Would you please move over?" And then we moved them across for a third time. By then the audience was getting resentful. But the herding was over, and they were in place to see the last piece, "See-Saw". And of course "See-Saw" ends with the Buffalo song. But since you've already read that one, just for now I offer a different song, one that I made up in high school:

> Talk about God and talk about soul
> I'm going to tell you
> 'bout an empty bowl
> It's empty.
>
> It's hugging around a lot of air
> And all that air was never there
> It's empty.
>
> And that there bowl it ain't there too
> It's never been there and neither have you
> It's empty.
>
> And while I'm here I'll say hello
> And why I do I'll never know
> I'm empty.

Early in the fall of 1961 I went to see Trisha Brown and Dick Levin. They were working together in the loft where I had done my dance constructions. They were dancing following sets of rules they had established. I joined them. Sometimes Steve Paxton worked with us. We developed many rule games, which we eventually performed as a concert. Trisha, Steve and I had all three attended Bob Dunn's composition course, and the rule games must have carried the influence of our exposure to chance operations. To this day I find working on rule games a good teaching tool.

OVER, UNDER AND AROUND

In this rule game the players alternate actions of going over, under and around each other, with visits to bases. A radio, tuned to any station, gives cues for when to change to the next kind of action or to the next base. Together, the players choose four bases. Each player decides privately which base will be his first, which his second, which his third, and which his fourth. If there are three players, each player has a repertoire of six actions: player A may go over player B, under player B, around player B, over player C, under player C, around player C. Each player decides privately the order in which he will do his action. For instance, player A may decide that his first action will be going under player B, his second going around player C, etc. He keeps his sequence constant throughout the game. Each player must alternate the performing of an action with the visit to a base. He must, however, continue to repeat the same kind of action and to keep returning to the same base until he hears his cue indicating that he is to proceed to his next kind of action or to his next base. Each player picks two letters as his cues, "e" and "f" for example. Whenever he hears, on the radio, a word beginning with the letter "e" he has to change to the next kind of action in his cycle. Until he hears another word beginning with "e" he must continue this kind of action between visits to a base. Whenever he hears a word beginning with the letter "f" he must begin to use the next spot in his base cycle. The action cycle and the base cycle will progress independently of each other. The player will find that the places in which he performs his actions will be determined by the wanderings of the other players. To visualize the general dynamics in this rule game, one must realize that often the cues come very quickly. And when you go to pass under someone, he may also be trying to pass under you, or over you, while the third player is trying to . . .

Malibu
L.A.
San Bernardino
Barstow
Las Vegas
St. George
Cedar City
Richfield
Green River
Grand Junction
Glenwood Springs
Golden
Denver
Limon
Burlington
Goodland
Colby
Oakley
Wa Keeney
Hays
Wilson
Salina
Junction City
Topeka
Lawrence
Kansas City

Columbia
Warrenton
St Louis
Effingham
Terre Haute
Brazil
Indianapolis
Richmond
Springfield
Columbus
Zanesville
Cambridge
Wheeling
Washington
Carlisle
Middletown
Norris Town
Elizabeth
Newark
Holland Tunnel
Manhattan

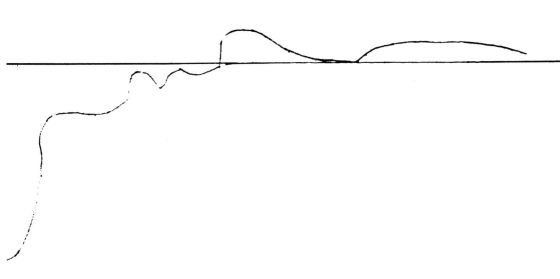

For two weeks I kept track of my perpendicular journey up and down buildings and subways. We were living on the sixth floor, I was teaching kindergarten on a sixth floor, and doing a lot of working, and rehearsing, and performing. During the whole of the second of the two recorded weeks, I was sick in bed. At the end of the two weeks I drew up a musical staff and placed the different stations up and down the scale. I came out with what I called an elevation tune. One day I handed the elevation tune to La Monte to hear what it sounded like. He whistled it to me, and in a palpable sense it had very much the feeling of those two weeks. It seemed to me that it was their ghost.

That week of being sick in bed had been a week of being suspended between two homes. Bob Morris and I had broken up. I married Bob Whitman. The elevation tune was the last piece I was to do for some time, for my interests turned to being a wife and right-hand helper in my husband's theater pieces, and trying to have a family.

Five years later, just by chance I decided to keep a record of the towns Whitman and I were driving through on a cross-country trip. I was making another elevation tune. I didn't know it then, but we were about to break up.

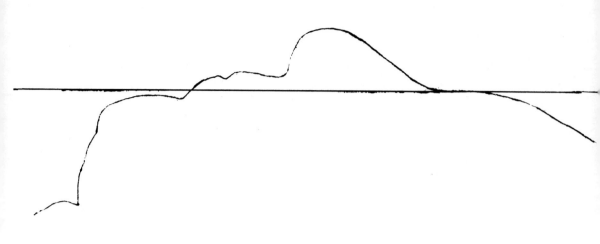

One Friday night I found myself in a roller rink in a black neighborhood in Washington, D.C. Everybody was skating around counter-clockwise, very fast. The music was playing, and while travelling very fast around the rink the skaters were also dancing very slowly, creating a double dynamic. The effect to me was of people whizzing by, and yet, when I focused on someone I would see him languidly dancing, almost in slow motion. The slightest movement of the spine would resonate and change the skater's trajectory through space. It was harmonics, resonating from centered action. A kind of graphics of the geometry of dynamics.

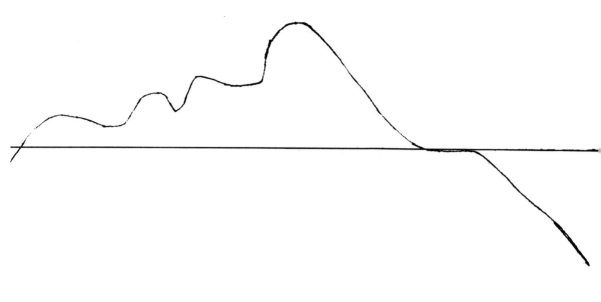

A friend introduced me to the I-Ching and the whole concept of
oracle. At first the appropriateness of the oracle would just about make
my hair stand on end. About this time I started smoking a lot of dope.
And the world view that had been my birthright started to blister and
curl, and to reveal itself as just one story among many others.

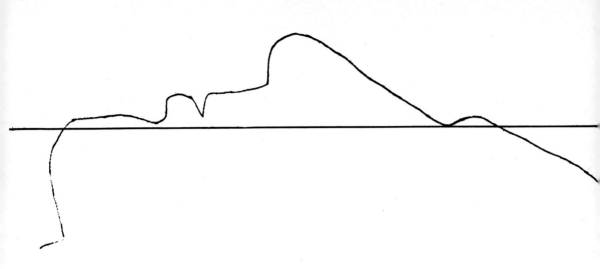

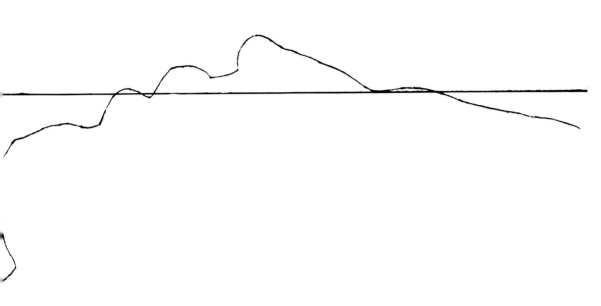

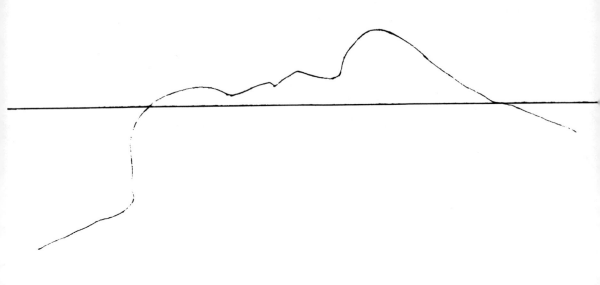

Though I've performed "Face Tunes" several times, I've never let the audience know they were listening to patterns derived from faces. I wanted people to listen to the music. I had faith that, since the awareness of variations among similar events is so basic a life process, when they heard "Face Tunes" they would unconsciously sense a familiar kind of order. As form seemed to be the storage place for presence, I hoped that the act of translating a coherent aspect of a set of faces to a corresponding form might awaken a more primitive level of pattern or ghost recognition.

77

zero Tone
Tape
line

motor

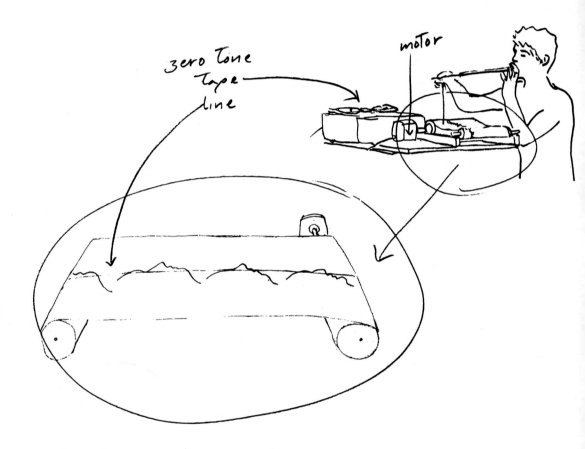

FACE TUNES

"Face Tunes" is a piece of music played from a score. The score is a set of outlines of seven profiles of faces traced on a long roll of paper. One straight line runs along the middle of the entire scroll. This is the zero line. The profiles face upwards, the throat of one followed by the forehead of another. The bridge of each nose sits on the zero line. The score is rolled on rollers turned by a motor, and the seven faces pass by, from left to right, at about one per minute. The performer sits in front of the score, holding a slide whistle. Attached to the end of the slide whistle is a stick that reaches down to the score. The player holds the whistle parallel to the score and plays it while tracing the profiles with the stick as the faces roll by. Simultaneously, a continuous tone is being played on the tape recorder. This constant pitch has been recorded from the slide whistle, and is the zero pitch. It is the pitch the slide whistle should be making when the stick is touching the zero line. Since the profiles are traced in higher and lower pitches, these are always in contrast with the zero pitch, except for periodic moments of convergence.

CLOTHS

This is a piece in which no one ever appears. There are three frames, of slightly different size and dimension, each large enough for someone to be crouching behind. On each frame there are four or five cloths stapled together to the top board, hanging on top of each other loosely covering the entire frame. The cloths are varied, collected from my friends. There are two tapes of songs. I recorded these by asking many friends to sing me their favorite song. I chose about eight that sounded the most like singing when you're hardly aware you're singing. The songs are spaced randomly, with silences between. There is a performer behind each of the three frames. As the piece begins, the cloths are hanging over the backs of their respective frames. Only the bottom-most cloth of each frame, a black one, is visible. The tapes begin. Along with the tapes, each performer sings a song from time to time. Periodically, from behind one of the frames a cloth is flipped over. There is a general overlapping of songs live and taped, interspersed with silences, and times when only one song is heard. The piece lasts about ten minutes, and within that time each performer must flip over his four or five cloths, and sing his two or three songs.

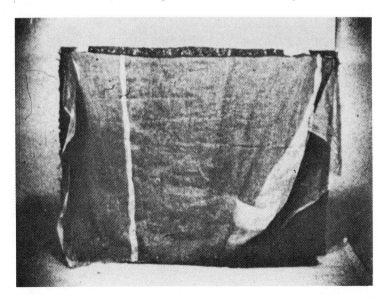

BOOK

This was a showing of a set of thirty-five black and white slides prefaced by a song. The song was a combination of two songs. I played the Beatles' "Fool on the Hill" on a record player, and at the same time I sang a very old Tuscan folksong. The two made a harmonious and amazing blend. The set of slides was an essay of brownie snapshots, made sometime earlier, mainly of images from my home with Whitman. The original format for the snapshots had been a notebook with one picture per page, presenting the images two by two. I projected them two by two, very large.

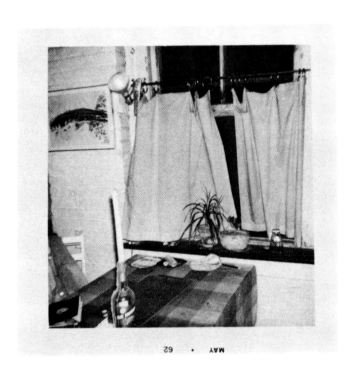

MAY • 62

83

showing of four slides together with four sections of sound

umming as frenetic and

nstant as possible,

ried by fatigue.

constant   chord held by

three voices: L.Y.,M.Z.,& S.F.

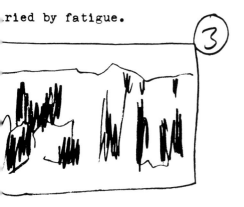

cum cleaner

following melodic line whisteled

repeatedly and feelingfully.

e slides were shown for five minutes each and the sections of sound lasted

ve minutes each, but the instant of transition from slide to slide and from

und to sound did not correspond exactly.

FALLERS

The concert took place in a seventeenth-floor penthouse. The terrace of the penthouse was illuminated. The audience was indoors, the lights out. Past the windows fell the performers, dropping twelve feet from penthouse roof to penthouse terrace, providing a glimpse of free-fall.

A young black man asked me to dance with him and said to me as we walked out onto the dance floor, "I'd like to see you dancing differently." I started trying to copy him. For a while my movements were very forced. I was trying to copy the outward form, and I wasn't getting it. Finally, I internalized the movement and I was dancing in a new way. In retrospect I find that this was my first experience at learning a new point of center in my movement. It was a matter of finding the right point of leverage, and of letting the momentums radiate and interface. The resonance between us in our dancing was deep and pure, and quite naturally we went home together.

In the late summer of 1968 I had a chance to go to Italy. In Rome I met Fabio Sargentini who accepted my proposal that I do a couple of concerts in his gallery, Galleria L'Attico. But somehow I no longer accepted my head as my workspace, and I didn't want to think up any new pieces. Fabio offered that as the gallery was open only in the afternoons and evenings, I could use it in the mornings as my studio.

Being a little lonely in an unfamiliar city, I took to spending a lot of time at the zoo. I found myself falling into a state of passive identification with the animals. You might say I was anthropomorphizing. But I'm sure that mind takes many forms, and as words are just a kind of notation, mind is in no way limited to verbal man. Those animals, too, were cut off from their natural environments, and in the zoo space even ear to foot had a different relationship to each other than when they were also in relation to the terrain with which they once formed a whole system. Yes, I felt a kinship with those encapsulated beings. In the afternoons, I watched them salvage, in their cages, whatever they could of their consciousness. In the mornings I worked alone on a dance called "Sleep Walkers." It was the first time in years that I allowed myself to be led by the feedback from my body sensations.

The dance eventually consisted of four movement studies. The first was inspired by the flamingos. I watched them tuck their head under one wing and, standing on one leg, go to sleep. It seemed so fantastic, that complete abandon, that easy, alert equilibrium on one leg. I was trying to go to sleep standing up. And for me, leaning backwards seemed to be a more likely way.

Another section was as close an adaptation as I could achieve of how the polar bear swings his head. The other two movements came from other sources — one came from the sea, and one from a happening I had once been in. But on the whole I was trying to achieve a kind of concentration that I found in some of the animals at the zoo, and I later came to think of "Sleep Walkers" as zoo mantras.

THROAT DANCE

This is a vocal improvisation in four sections. I limited myself to four types of vocal sounds, doing an improvisation on each. Each section had its own place in the room. One sound type was my very highest threshold of pitch. It is a matter of getting a great degree of constriction in the throat and increasing the air pressure very gradually until it just passes the threshold of being able to pass through the constriction. I can't keep this balance of pressure and constriction constant, but I do my best, producing a flutter of clear, piercing squeaks. Another type was a loud double sound achieved with a throat posture that must be close to purring. The third was rhythmic pitch leaps, and the fourth of a similar order.

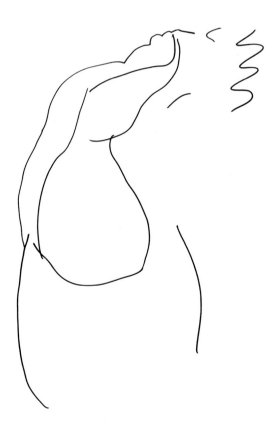

I spent the winter in Turin, where I was part of a theater group called The Zoo. There was a writer, an artist, a musician, I was a dancer, and there were many other people. One of the directors of the Turin branch of the Italian State Theater wanted to include some unconventional work in the next season's repertoire, and commissioned us to do a play. As an American I assumed that now all we had to do was simply set our sights on doing a performance. For the Italians it was quite a different matter. Turin is an industrial city. As I understand it, some art-collecting Fiat executives had rented a large garage and invited many local artists to use it as their studio space. Shortly after the artists had moved in, Pasolini was scheduled to do a play there and the artists were kicked out. The play took place amidst a boycott. After the play, the garage being empty, our group, The Zoo, began using it for rehearsals.

Meanwhile, I was teaching a movement workshop for the apprentices to the State Theater. I had assumed that as choreographer for the Zoo I would bring my students with me into the play. Our writer, however, refused to let them join us. He argued that it was immoral of me to be teaching through the State Theater, the streets being the only place where anything honorable can be learned. There were many other stormy periods. The director who had invited us in the first place was himself no longer in very good standing with the State Theater. One day he asked me to do a demonstration of a class with the movement workshop for a social club. I did it. Our writer was so angered with me that he withdrew his script. The play never came off. However, in terms of gestures, it had been a successful event, and everyone seemed to have come through with reasonable honor. I remained the confused American.

I gave some thought to whipping out a concert of my own work, but finally decided against it. All that came of the idea is this jingle:

> Buffalo Bill, what did you kill?
> I saw the herd, but as I shot the third
> My friends kicked me in the bird.
> How absurd!

The sudden disorientation of a fatal wound. Before the pain. That's the moment of death. It hovers over - in - some beautiful faces.

'improvvisa disorientazione di una ferita fatale... prima del dolore. È questo il momento di morte che ombreggia in qualche faccie molti belle.

Feb 6

Went back to the Egyptian
museum. Last time i was
there i'd kissed a sarcofagus
on the mouth. i did again
today, the same one. it's mouth
is very beautiful. i kissed his
it very fleetingly because i don't
want to be discovered by the guard.
Perhapse in part because of my
rush and timidity, the kiss
felt very real. If i'd been alone
i'd have bent over for a second
kiss. But instead i did line
my face up with the face on
looked at it as i'd look at a
mans face, doing the eye thing
It's expressions kept changing
as i became ¥ aware of
formations. It was as if we
were reading each others
faces.

And if none of this is true it's OK
↓
(that i'm a witch, that there are witches)

But it's because i'm writing it that it'll be
O.K. for me if it's not True
My dream (that i'm a witch) will not come True
But i'm so happy at seeing this connection
that i don't Knowtice the pain. And i
pretend to act as if i thought my dream
comming true. Because i was a clown (one
who sees the edge of a gesture, Well if i'm
not a witch, i'm a clown.

_____

remembering some -
AGt the I-King). If i do think
it works, i won't try to water
down my style by looking
for scientific explanations
I just kick it. I just
give the I-King a kick
like you would a radio
It's too funny. It's strong,
that. The I-King or being a

Le risposte uccidono

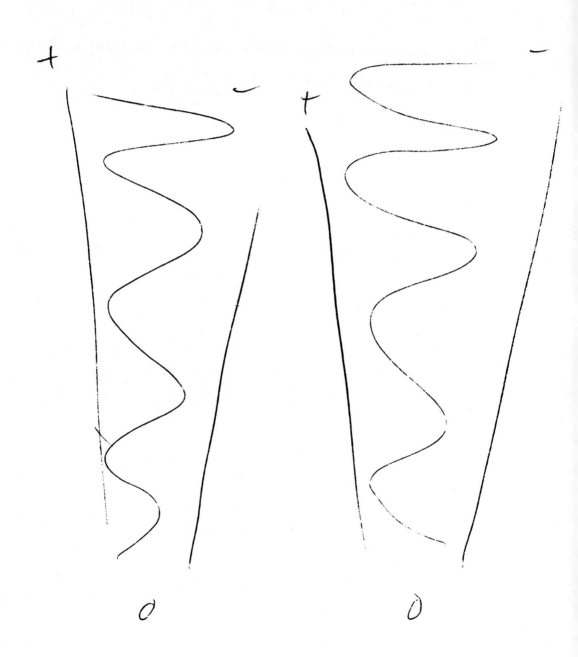

Answers kill.

The more you learn to trust
your automatic pilot
The more crucial and basic
choices you let him make
and the more his mistakes
could be fatal.
But the better you fly.
And at great speeds
he takes over anyway.

The next summer I took part in Fabio Sargentini's Rome Festival of Music, Dance, Explosion and Flight.

It is true. I was stoned. Very beautiful day. And in some ways a moment of glory for me. Fabio had placed a lot of faith in me, and I had been a major force in setting things up. I was fluent in both English and Italian, and a lot of communication had to pass through me. Everything I touched was falling into place. I had my mojo going. We all parked our cars at the side of the highway and took the trail through the tall grass, towards the pond where the explosion was going to take place. I took a detour with a few friends to where we could drop out of sight as La Monte passed the pipe. Around the pond we were an elegant bunch. The women in long skirts and mini-skirts and pants. The photographers in black. The men licensed to do theatrical explosions were wading and swimming in the water, setting the charges. I sat with Anna, and watched her infant daughter as she lay in the fragrant shade of a parasol. There were going to be a couple of small test explosions before the main one. The jolt. The water rising. The report. Then people looking into the water. Photographers shooting into the water. The fish were coming up dead. I walked over to David Bradshaw and asked him if, in the light of the dying fish, he felt that one explosion had been enough. He said, or so I remember, that the death of the fish was not the intention of the piece, and that he would continue. Right. I squatted beside a tree, my head in my hands. Another jolt, water rising not watched, report. It is true. I was stoned and I was watching the ants at my feet. They were going crazy. Through their frenetic scrambling I had a vision of their ancient tunnels crumbling. My tears fell among them. And I was miles into the sky. And these tiny forms were people down below, scrambling on the surface of their crumbling survival structure. Radial victims of a linear intent. It is true. I was stoned. I was there, but I was not in Rome. I was with the ants.

A couple of months later I was at the Woodstock Festival, fully believing that I had forever abandoned the sheath of surface tension that seemed to separate my identity from the rest of the universe of flux in time and space.

In retrospect, I've come to think that the strangest part of my Woodstock experience is that I had no sense of how it was based on conditions of economic privilege. We thought we were surfing the rainbow flow to a golden, all-inclusive, continuing orgasm. But we were flowing through channels of national economic surplus. Riding on checks from home, on gifts, scavenging and finding a wealth of refuse. It was beautiful, and it left us free to explore many ways. But it wasn't the messianic vision I took it to be. I could have found my way from a psychedelic commune to a working commune. But I didn't. When I've referred to David Bradshaw's dynamite piece it seems I'm pointing a finger at him. That's ironic. It's David who told me about hunting, and about how still you have to become in the woods before you are part of its motion and can see and judge what to do. And I trust he knew what he was doing. And it's David, not I, who made a real move to disengage himself from the centralized system, living and working with his friends and family in the mountains of Vermont.

When I got to California I had returned from far away. What I brought with me was a longing to be an intimate witness to the graphics of dynamic equilibrium, and a longing to look into the eyes.

A real change had taken place in me. I was seeking a teaching job, but I refused to pull out my old credentials, i.e. the name I had once made for myself. In certain ways, the whole question of being an artist was still suspect. It's hard for me to remember, because my thinking continues to change. But I must try to remember. There was a time, in New York, when I felt in competition with other dancers, with other artists, and had a competitive sense of identity. And dancing functioned, to a great extent, defined within that way of sensing identity. One aspect of my work was that it invented ground. In fact, part of my grid of requirements was to invent ground. Was to invent . . . how can I say it? . . . people know it, but, even so, it's better if I can say it. Was to invent a relationship of need to mind, to manifestation. To invent a new house, a new structure of relationships of those things.

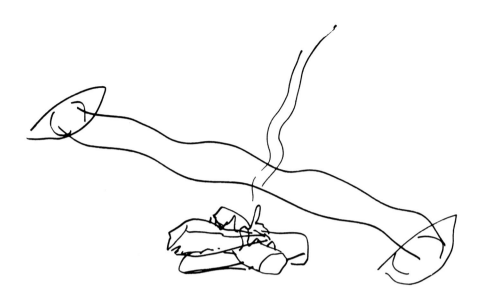

The circle   we are one around the fire

After Woodstock I held all that suspect. In a way I had started holding it suspect in Italy. I think of the dynamite piece that David Bradshaw did in Rome as the moment in my life when I clearly realized how much I had begun to doubt the way that had been my way and that I shared with a lot of artists. I couldn't understand, but I sensed a common world view between an aesthetic research coming out of New York and the foreign policy coming out of Washington.

The requirements that a piece would have to fulfill somehow suddenly seemed very narrow. And in order to get at how it was that they seemed narrow, I think of a book I once read on the Hopi. According to them, the world has been destroyed four times. They speak of a pair of twins, each stationed at one of the earth's poles. The twins watch over the vibrational line that goes from pole to pole, which is the earth's sounding center. And it's at this sounding

This can not be.
why can this not be?

Oct 70

freeway

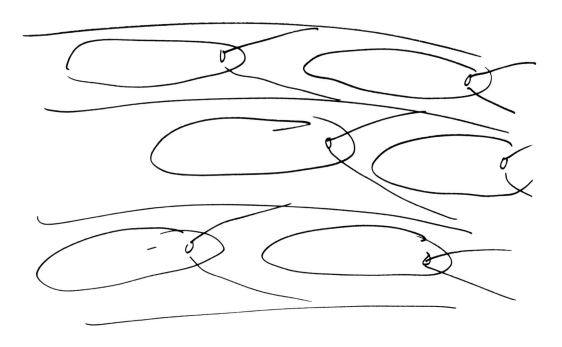

center that the earth is in contact with the vibrations of the rest of the universe. The people are in tune with this sounding center through the tops of their heads. So the question is one of keeping the top of your head open. The Hopi speak of themselves as a people who have a migration to complete, and their pattern of migration has taken them spiralling around both American continents, keeping on the move for generations. As they migrated, they could sometimes stop to take advantage of a couple of years of growing crops in one place. But the temptation was to remain stationary, and to grow into a city. Life is easier that way, and, also, in a large stable community one can become known, make a name for oneself. The danger in that is its tendency to cause the tops of peoples' heads to close. And when the tops of peoples' heads close, the poles of the earth reverse and the world is destroyed. The first time the world was destroyed it was by fire. A few people who still had the tops of their heads open saw the sign that the end of the world was coming. The sign was a cloud, which they followed. They followed this cloud for a long time, until they came to a place where there was a hole in the earth. They went down into the hole, as the cloud told them to, and the ant people took them in. I forget how long they stayed down there, maybe four days, maybe six. Anyway, while they were down there with the ant people the world was destroyed by fire. Then they came out of the hole . . . and the whole thing starts all over. The people keep migrating, then they gather in cities, and the tops of their heads shut, and the world is destroyed again.

It seemed to me that in New York my grid requirements had been structured by certain elements of human potential, of human function, of life function. But in a sense it tended towards closed systems. It lacked certain channels of openness to systems we cannot comprehend. Cannot comprehend in a comprehensive way, but which we do have access to, and which we play part mind of.

We've all gone through times of every morning waking up scared. That's how it was for me then. And yet by the time I'd be standing in the middle of the room I wouldn't be scared anymore. I had a good life. I was living with old friends in a big house, and I had reasonable plans. I had decided to reinstate myself in the "world". Among my

106

plans was doing a concert and getting a job teaching.

It's not surprising that the trouble I was having was showing itself in that moment of passage from sleep to wakefulness. For in my happy new life I was more and more turning my back on the life that in Woodstock I thought I had embraced forever. Turning my back on the life I had lived and preached with a kind of Bible-thumping energy. Turning my back on my fantasy of someday bringing my grandchildren into the ruins of the city to dig up some needed pieces of metal, and there, as an old woman, telling them about the days I could still remember when there had been gasoline-powered vehicles, and people had lived in cubicles in strange, tall buildings, leaving their homes at a time designated by the number nine and returning at five. And now, it seemed that in one short month that Utopian myth had all but faded into mist, and I could hardly remember it.

I focused a lot of energy on Tai Chi. This study acted as a bridge between my stoned head and my straight head. It's hard to say how this was, but it was. Tai Chi is a discipline distilled from centuries of understanding, and yet it seemed to speak to the matters which concerned me when I was stoned. Maybe what appealed so much to my spirit was the combination of a close-up view of the very grain of dynamics, together with a sense of sensibleness and a clear position of personal will. During many of his classes, Marshall Ho'o, the instructor, would talk for fifteen or twenty minutes. His talks cast a lot of light on the world view from which Tai Chi comes, but they were always direct communications of his own thinking about movement. And Marshall has thought a great deal about movement. He would talk to us about the things he most wondered about. Listening to his thoughts was not only interesting to me, it was vital. I learned a lot from him about what I might call the biology of movement, the politics of movement, and movement as a living model of the ways of The Way. I found that I could work on Tai Chi with the same absorption with which in my days in Woodstock I used to sit and watch the fire. In practising every day I was making friends with my inner strength. And I was developing a degree of ease and control in my movement that I had never before known and that eventually became the base for my own dancing.

What?   What?
Wisely
A few twigs were left
For the old
To throw into the fire

I would visit all the places I have left
Then I would know myself differently

Bank the fires

I missed all the dancing I'd been doing in Woodstock. So I gave a lot of thought to the kind of dancing I now wanted to do, and to how I could create the conditions for this kind of dancing to happen. I think there's a state of dancing, like there's a state of sleeping, or a state of shivering. Some people have a shyness towards entering that state, but everybody does it sometime. Often, at parties, people drop their shyness and enter a dance state. And when I'm in a dance state, the movement that comes out through me enchants me. It can be very simple movement, but it always comes with a sense of wonder, and as one of life's more delicious moments. Melodies are like that, too. They just come. God knows from where.

So I wanted to find my way again to often being in a dance state. And I wanted to apply a great deal of energy to making a serious study of that state, and of the movement that came to me in it. I started out by trying to find people to dance and make music with. Mainly I was trying to do this from my home base in the school cafeteria. I would talk to people, and, whenever it seemed that they too wanted to get together and jam, we would decide on a place and time. But often, although our words around the table indicated that we could and should work together, when we actually tried it was not so. And enough of us were frustrated in this way that the potential for an in practice meeting ground was there. So I proposed Open Gardenia.

The proposal for Open Gardenia had two main points. One, that we needed an open market-place where people could find each other. Two, that such an open market-place was especially needed by those of us who were studying any of the ancient, non-Western musics and movement arts that were being offered at the institute. For, though we were deeply involved in these non-Western arts, we continued to work in our own tradition of individual search and invention. I felt that we reflected a larger, grass-roots receptivity to more communal and non-Western musical attitudes, and that we needed each other if we were going to make any progress towards finding some common-denominator base of operations.

The proposal was accepted. We could use a certain room every Friday night. Open Gardenia was ready to manifest itself, and it took life. And every Friday night I could work on the kind of movement that most interested me. I was going in a circle a lot. I was a forming element of one sort, and other people were forming elements of other sorts. Sometimes people would get tired of it and stop coming. I felt that if I myself could just keep going, if I could just get through two real tired Friday nights, then the next Friday night would start regaining life. And that's exactly how it happened.

Fri Nov 12 Open Gardenia
We must thank the spirits.
Very beautiful. (Poster just a page
out of small red notebook. Again on
caffeteria buletin board.) Paul set
the lights long befor Gardenia
hour. I could see them from
outside the caffeteria. Colored
lights .. soft and bright. As
I approached the door of
C105 I could hear a droar
The Bukla cynthecizer. People
started comming. I recognized
the flute player and the
tamboura player from last
week. Vickey played some
little clear bells. I sang a
drone... a few of us sang

drones ... with some soft
and regular variations.
As many as twenty or so
people came. Everyone
listened very well. Made
room for each others sound.
The sound stayed soft
for about 45 min or so.
Mabe an hour. Then the
spirit swelled and many
high spirited waves of
music and dancing. I
got a chance to do a
lot of heavy hand spinning.
There was a lot of dancing.
Very free and beautiful. Some-
imes we were like flying ...

skipping.. running... in
circles concentric and in
both directions.. passing
each other at a flying
pace. We made music
and danced till 10.

Thank you

also for the
beautiful rain
last night.

I dream that these improvisations are part of a process that leads through generations, from unmanifest grass-roots to a highly evolved communal tradition. As in India. A tradition that can house the collaboration of limitless numbers of initiates. As in Jazz. The common ground must happen inductively. Not in one mind, but through an organic sifting. I feel that this kind of process can happen in dancing, and to a large extent it has happened. Americans are dancers. Strange, but true. Many white Americans are assimilating patterns that have come from Africa, getting their first experience of harmonic movement. The thread from Africa is only one of many. And the roots of our common store of movement lie in our various roots and in our common experiences. These include the workshop, the rock festival, the museum, the kindergarten, the ballroom, the party. And the land itself. For I think that a continent holds its own potential for kinds of movement that will manifest on its surface. While concept can't begin the process of synthesis, an Open Gardenia can participate in the formation of a tradition.

With making pieces, too, there arises a general agreement on the arena of discourse, forming the matrix for all the exceptions. And each piece must be an exception. With the pieces the process of agreement can be faster, the capsule form of the pieces lending itself so well to single-minded coherence. The pieces are like water that, covering trees in an ice storm, stands in the air. The dancing can seek its level, slowly carving channels inherent in the land. Perhaps I've shied away from the pieces because just now I love the dancing more, and because the pieces always come to me with that acrid smell from under my arms that in high-school used to warn me that I was about to raise my hand to set everybody straight on any issue at hand. And that smell pinpoints for me the fact that if I ever felt any conflict between being a woman and being an artist, it's been in the dimension of what might be my endocrine balance. Finally, it has nothing to do with engaging in creative pursuits in itself but with the hormonal posture that seems to accompany being a professional artist in our society.

It's early fall now in Nova Scotia, the days are bright and cool, the grass in my back yard is still green. Nearly every day I practice Tai Chi, and I'm vaguely aware of figures stopping for a moment,

113

watching, and moving on. My mind is void of all but the practice, interspersed with feelings, thoughts, and impressions. And it's true, I do feel some pride, and I do feel that I bring this form to the neighbourhood, and that it's something the neighbourhood has. Like a brook. The other day I was aware of a small boy sitting in the grass a way off, watching, lost in thought.

One day I was having dinner at Nam June Paik's house. He was talking about one of the classical histories of China. He picked up a volume and started translating the page it opened to. The story was about a king and a master musician. The king commanded the musician to play for him the saddest music in the world. The musician refused, saying that the king was not ready to hear it, and that therefore it would be disastrous. But the king insisted. The musician played, and the king was overwhelmed by the beauty of the music. When the musician stopped playing, he told the king he had not played the very saddest music in the world. The king insisted again on the very saddest, and again the musician refused, repeating that the king was not ready to hear it and that it would be disastrous for the entire kingdom. But still the king insisted. As the musician started to play, three dark cranes appeared in the sky, and flew down to the gates of the palace. At this point Nam June closed the book. I don't know the rest of the story.

A basic principle of Tai Chi is the sinking of the ch'i *(life force) to a point below the navel. This point should be the point of mass integration of all movement.*

It is said of a certain great Tai Chi master that if a fly landed on his arm he could render it unable to fly away simply by dropping his arm in exact proportion to the fly's push-off.

Once I was looking into the face of a black brother as he heard that the F.B.I. was looking for him. I clearly remember the movement of his eyes. To begin with, he looked straight ahead to such a distance that the beams of his two eyes were parallel. Then, the left eye holding constant, the right eye moved sideways to a forty-five-degree angle.

I remember a dance I saw in Hotevilla, an ancient Hopi pueblo. It was a line dance, it was a couple dance, the boys and girls alternating down the line. The adult men were singing. At a certain refrain the boys would turn and each would find himself facing a girl. The boys would step facing to one side, let's say to the east, while the girls would step facing to the west. Then the boys would step facing to the west and the girls to the east. And they would go back and forth three or four times while glancing at each other's faces. At this point it always seemed to me that they were just about to start giggling, but it would be time for the boys to face forward and the whole line would go on.

proposal: 1 = pi

Some months ago at a party, I tried to tell Emmett Williams about a problem I was having in making this book. I felt that in Woodstock I had shared in a certain vision. And if I was going to talk about dancing, to a great extent it was going to be in the context of that vision. My ways were meeting with a lot of resistance. So it seemed that I couldn't do the book without translating the vision. And I didn't know how to do that. What's more, I was afraid that some demon was going to get me. Emmett listened to me, and nodded, and put on a record of dogs barking "Jingle Bells".

Several months ago, at a party, I tried to tell Emmett
about a problem I was having in making this book. I
guess I was feeling that up to the time of doing acid
I had seen the world in a certain way. Then, with
acid, I had seen other things. And I didn't know how
to correlate these two visions. I didn't know how to
throw a net of words over this problem. And I felt
that if I did manage to exploit my stoned vision in the
service of my streight vision, I would be made to pay
a fearfull price. Emmett listened to me and nodded,
said "just a minute", and put on a record of dogs
barking Jingle Bells.

As I've worked on this book, I've kept expecting a
system to form in my mind. I think that the acid had
polarized my perceptions. I was recognizing patterns
which previously I had left unrecognized. To my
amazment, it seemed that the somatic threshold decisio-
ns of whether to contract or expand were a common root
of both perception and the orgasm. And somewhere in
that maze seemed also to be the story on magic and on
the oracle as a reading of the pulse of the moment.

The whole question of measurement seems to lie at the
center of what I'm trying to understand. When I was
in college, I attended a teacher education course called
New Math. The emphasis was on the fact that to percieve
properties of quantity is one thing. To make notes of
these perceptions is an other. And to manipulate
notation is still another. But even the materials which
the children handled to obtain their first hand
perceptions of aspects of quantitative variation
seemed to be modled after the standard ideal foot long
rod. Absolute position seemed to be the underlying
assumption reguarding what constituted perception
of quantitative variation.

I understand Duchamp's Three Standard Stopages as
reference units which are less arbitrary then the
meter or the yard. But there seems to be nothing
arbitrary about harmonic breakdown. In the Raga,
an ancient musical form of India, the tamboura holds
a droan. The droan breaks into harmonics and, being
constant, provides a grid in relation to which the voice
moves. The voice and its harmonics must be in
phase with the droan. This is achieved by compensating for all the forces acting to disrupt this
state of dinamic equilibrium. I've always felt that

a droan could never be recorded. It is exactly
specific to its live time and to all the elements
of that moment. It requires the immediate living facu
lty of perception and compensation. As a point of
equilibrium it does not seem to admit to absolute
position or to lend itself to agreed upon notation.
When the mind's eye stays focused on that situation
of equilibrium, the active compensations become a
negative mirror of the world and a way of being in
touch with things that one can not encompase with
ones conceptual structure.

Also in college, I was reading about experimental
psychology and learned to take for granted the
method of studying one element of behavior by setting
up two situations which would be considered identical.
One situation would be held constant whilein the other
the facter in question would be somehow altered and the
unfolding of both situations would be compared. It seems
to me that my early pieces come out of this climate.
The Huddle and the Slantboard are each a unit
defined by its own uniformity of process. They are more
closed systems that not, arrived at by abstracting and
reordering elements of one situation to create
another which is of a new order. The elements of the
situation are elements of its defenition and of
cultural agreement.

In the western musical scale the intervals are positioned
so as to avoid a predominance of the natural harmonic
breakdown of tones. I've wondered if systems based
on organically arbitrary units tend to reinforce a
territoriality of exclusive space through an arangemenT
of vibrational disinfectants. And I wonder If certain
functions can atrophy causing an imbalance in the
powers that reside in the human animal. And if the
precarious state of health of the ocean can be a resulT
of a disproportionate development of the powers that
come of standardized measurement.

It seems to me that when the polar bear swings his
head, he is in a dance state. He is in a state of
establishing measure, and of communion with the forces
of which he is part.

One day I talked to Les about my two apparently
different images of what the world must be. I
used the words "conceptual" and "vibrational".
I wasn't clear about what I was thinking, I'm not
clear about what he said. But one clue came through
to me. I think he said something like "You can just
follow harmonics, and you can keep doing that until
you run into a barier." And this started me thinking
about conceptualization as a tool for choosing
the dementions in which to place those bariers which
do and must exist. There are harshnesses involved in
lasting from season to season. Each culture seems
to deal with this complex of harshnesses with its own
particular complex of definitions, measurements, and
controlls. Control over birth, over territory, over
incest, control over killing, control over succomming
to death. Each of these control networks is reflected
in and aided by that culture's movement conventions,
Placement of center is one key to the survival
network. Rythmic structure is a n other key. For
the body has a different geometry and measures ~~it~~
differently in time according to at what point along
the spine is located the center of movement. The
movement that has come to me from ancient America,
from Africa, and from Asia, has come as systems of
relating to the dua lity that life support seems to
imply as a competitive struggle against entropy.
One principle of Tai Chi that has very much interested
me, prescribes the way in which an opposing force is
to be met. One must not counteroppose with ones own
force, but simply pivot on ones own center just
slightly deflecting the opposition and letting it fly
past of its own momentum.

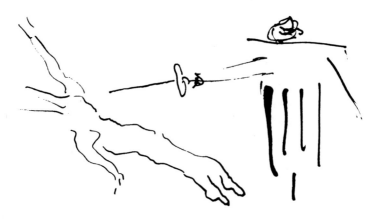

shouting aT

The waffe

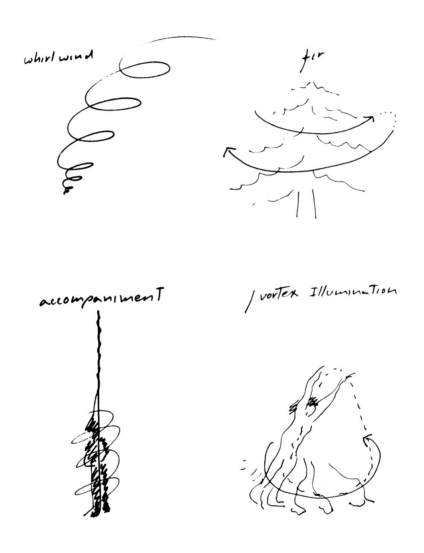

whirl wind

fir

accompaniment

/ vortex Illumination

123

Tuning measures

finding

measure

measure

measure

measure

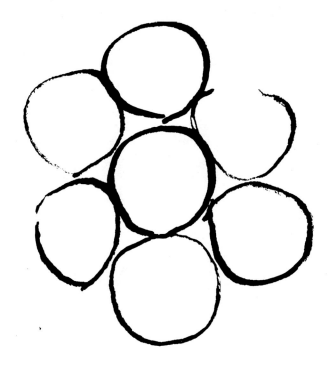

I dreamed that I was balancing on the edge of a pit. In one hand I held a baby by the arm. I could get my weight over solid ground only by using the baby as counterbalance and I could get the baby over solid ground only by using myself as counterbalance. I twisted and squirmed as I clung to our deteriorating equilibrium. When I awoke it seemed to me that I could have simply lowered my center of balance.

I once read in an article on the history of dance that originally the Hebraic sacred scriptures had been sung by a dancing chorus, but that over the years this way had fallen out of favor. There was the dancing around the golden calf, and generally the union of dancing and worship came to be seen as a pagan phenomenon. Eventually the scriptures were still sung, but with feet held fast.

Charlemagne and I met when we were both trying to set up a concert in California for Pandit Pran Nath. At that time I was sounding out every musician I ran into about whether we shouldn't be working together. Charlemagne and I found that we could concentrate in one another's presence, and that we shared the attitude of standing by and nurturing whatever might be the fruit of our concentration. The college had a very large music hall with a fine hardwood floor, a high ceiling, and a great deal of resonance. We took to working in there, calling it the Temple.

I find it interesting to realize that the word "enchant" shares the same root with the word "chant". I've mentioned what I call the dance state. In a way, it's a state of enchantment. Perhaps it's a state of polarization into harmonic channels along which motor energy pleasurably flows. When I'm dancing, I am moved by that mysterious response to the music. And I pursue that special order of thoughts that come out of the body in motion and which seem to be one with the motion itself.

The aspect of Charlemagne's music that most inspired my imagination was his melodies. Sometimes their texture of repetitions and evolving variations are so close that the term melody doesn't seem to apply. But the pitch combinations seem to draw their integrity from the organic sympathy that exists between the throat and the heart. His predominant time sense is a kind of ongoingness. The time unit seems to stem from pitch, or wave length, and from the recurrences emerging in the developing patterns of wave reinforcements and interferences. What most determined our format was Charlemagne's way of letting the elements in the music develop only very gradually.

Our ritual for starting a session was simply to start very slowly and very simply. Any sound that went out, the walls echoed back, and in exchange for careful listening, offered a dynamic clarity. I would usually just walk for a long time, circling in that clear space, tuning my efforts till the ongoing momentum of my whole mass came into clear feeling focus. And I developed a gliding kind of striding.

An important element that Charlemagne and I had in common was that we had both worked for a short time with Pran Nath. This gave us a clear, common point of reference — an approach that begins

129

130

with perfecting a pitch until it is a pure and constantly coherent vibration. In order to arrive at a pure vibration one must develop the ability to sustain the necessary balance of the physical elements involved. And in order to do this, a centering, a state of calm receptivity, is necessary. Once a pure pitch is established as a fine point of dynamic balance, its harmonics become clearly manifest.

Pran Nath has compared the state of mind at the time of singing to the flame of a candle. If there is any disturbance in the mind or in the environment, the flame will flicker. I imagine that he was speaking in terms of protecting the flame from disturbance. But the image helps me understand something else which I feel must be related. When I achieve precisely regular intonation of balance shifts, any kind of breeze passing through my field of consciousness will touch off my center of balance, and variations of form will reverberate as shadows of that breeze. When Charlemagne and I work together he centers through pitch and I center through balance. And his sound and my movement form part of each other's effective environment, which gives motion to our equilibriums.

One of the first kinds of balance that I explored in our sessions was walking on a very narrow line. I became aware that there was a point in my center around which there seemed to be a lateral circle of mirrors. In order for me to maintain equilibrium, each shift had to somehow be mirrored in its opposite direction. The mirroring would not be an exact opposite, but an evolvement of shape and momentum that had equivalent weight. I wasn't doing this in a studied way, it was simply a mechanism of intelligence that I found existing in my body. I sensed that I had hit on an organic set of links between mind, balance, and gesture, and it seemed that here was the basis for a natural language. Sometimes, having achieved a state of balance, I would lift my eyes up and to the right as if saying hello. The sudden asymmetry would take me by surprise and the resultant internal careening of my center seemed to radiate into an outburst of a kind of song whose melody was made of movement. And I would find myself weaving movement melodies charged with stories the body holds.

Perhaps my perpetual circling came as a natural resolution between the desire to propel myself continuously, and the reality of working

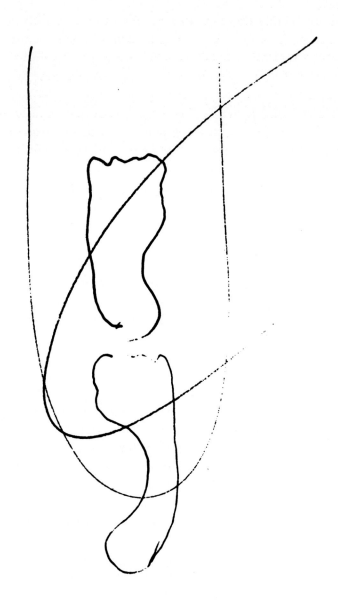

speaking

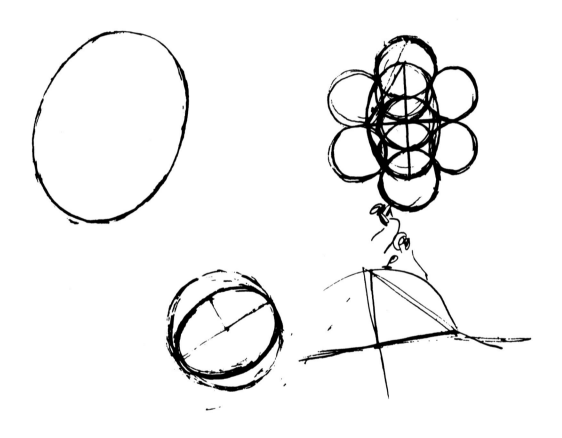

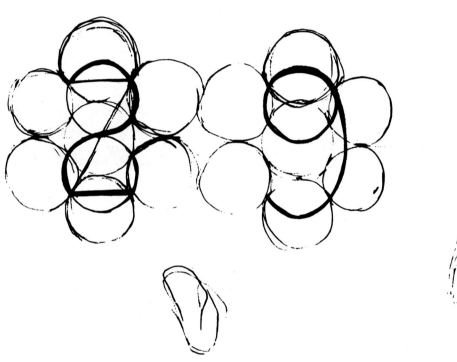

26
25

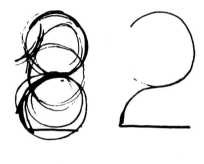

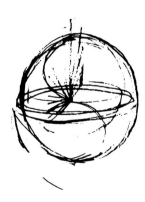

in an inclosed space. I've seen monkeys circling in their cages. But I've also seen dogs circling on open fields. And certainly, the dynamics of circling are wonderful to manipulate. I started working on an action in which, as I exhale, I give in to centripetal force. And as I inhale, well, I don't know what it is, maybe my center rises, but suddenly I'm much more under the sway of centrifugal force. And I loop in and out of the circle on my way round and round. If I allow a kind of a whiplash in my spine, it effects my trajectory, compounding an S form into the repetitive wave patterns. If I extend my inhalation as far as I can, I find myself in a dynamic eddy just at the very edge of the circle, and I can drift into a backwards loop before exhaling and being again drawn towards the center and going on. I found that if I stepped very quickly round and round a small circle I could lean very steeply in towards its apex. Almost strangely so. And it seemed that I could isolate nearly all the effort to my legs, and that I could abandon most of my weight to a waving flame-like energy that seemed to be rising up the center of the vortex.

These formations are easy to indicate in words. And in dancing, they're easy for me to remember and to return to. But they only form a kind of skeletal structure for the live movement, for the live thought.

I was developing an interest in drawing circles, and was training my hand to the proportions of the seven circles which form the basis of the Star of David and of the Arabic numerals. In my dancing I was banking from orbit to orbit. And whereas in banking I was identifying a high center with the precarious dynamics of circumference, in practicing Tai Chi I was learning to identify a low center with the stable dynamics of center. In rock dancing I had sifted out of the music the necessity of bouncing the center of balance, patterning it up and down the spine. And somehow, within the field of Charlemagne's music, my automatic pilot could give vent to many different structural attitudes, revealing some of the harmonics of a continent crossed by many migrations. And I pondered the idea that I was involved in a kind of dynamology.

Often, before starting a work session, I would smoke a joint. And the first three performances that Charlemagne and I did, I was stoned. But I was finding myself afraid. The geometry that was coming out

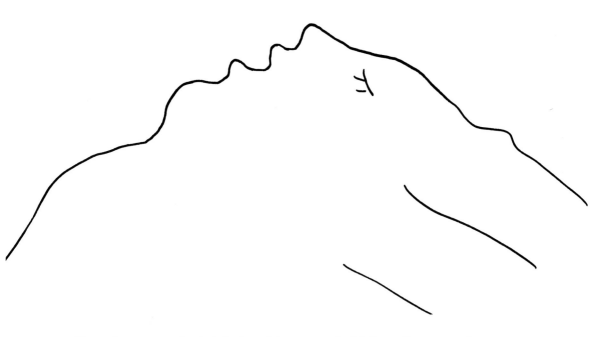

through me was absolutely knocking me out. At times I was running into veritable demons. I seemed to be tapping into something powerful, and I didn't know to what extent I was the wilful element. I was questioning my motives. I was teaching a workshop and felt that what my students needed to see of me was how I could get it together out of my own artistry. What can I say? I got my omens and heeded them. It was hard because I was afraid that I had gotten deep into movement to which I had sure access only when I was stoned. And at first it was harder and I did have access to less, but it was enough. Some aspects were clearer and I focused on those and instead of having to abandon an overextended position, I was able to solidify a base of recurrent movement studies. I must add that all this time Charlemagne was working straight. Or if he had an ally, it was brandy. The demons are his old friends.

By then I was living in the Sunkist orange groves. On my way to the post office one day, I cut through a neighbor's yard and was challenged by their dog. Before I knew what I was doing, I had squared my stance and had flung a return challenge. It was accepted. I ran backwards all the way out of the yard, stopping twice to renew my threat, giving myself, in the dog's momentary startlement, the edge that got me out of range just in time. That same day, stopping my car

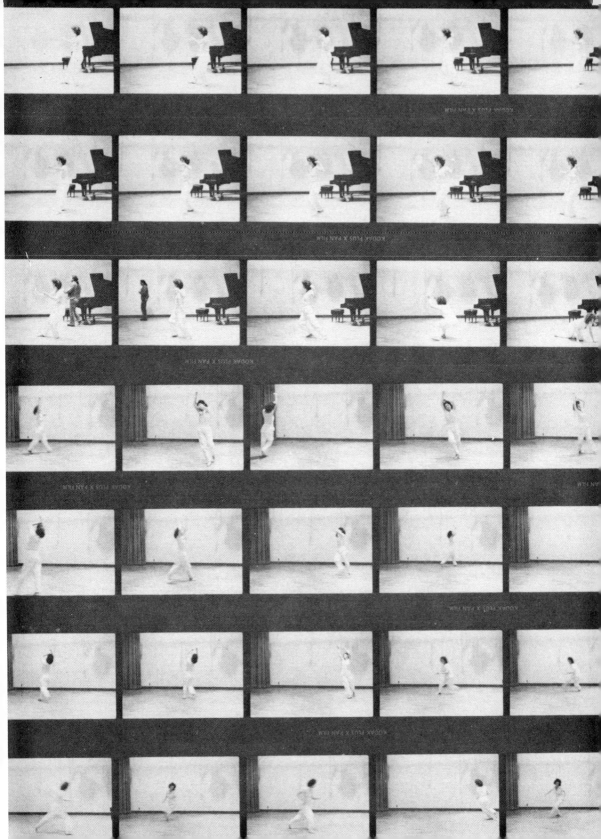

by a stream, I walked to the water's edge. A great beautiful dog came bounding up, wanting to play. He grabbed my wrist in his teeth, not hard enough to hurt, but not letting go either. I disengaged my wrist, swatting him on the nose, and it seemed to him like a good game. It was no use, he wasn't going to let me be. I returned to my car, his teeth on my wrist, swat, teeth on my wrist, swat.

In my next sessions with Charlemagne I started working on a movement that was a combination of being suddenly interrupted in my banking by the teeth on the wrist, sharply swatting the nose, and running precipitously backwards. In other words, shouting at the wolf. This movement appeared like the sharp breath of cedar smoke. And in my vortex riding, falling, falling, never falling, I started crossing the threshold and crashing to the ground. And I started crawling.

Often in concerts I have sung songs, one or two, maybe four or five songs. Singing on my way around the circle. One song I sing always gets me running in a large figure-eight, or in a large circle, moving my arms in such a way that I'm propelled in a spiral along its outer edge:

I look around me and I see goodwill
And I look inside me and I see goodwill
But the spots of blindness they linger still
To tilt the wheel to tilt the wheel

And did we fly to earth or will we fly away
Did we fly to earth or will we fly away
And a song of choosing where to go
Is a song of wonder
A song of wonder
Full song of wonder

And the endless summer rolls on and on
And forever clockwise it's spun and spun
And forever counter it's spun and spun
And the endless winter rolls on and on

And did we fly to earth or will we fly away

139

140

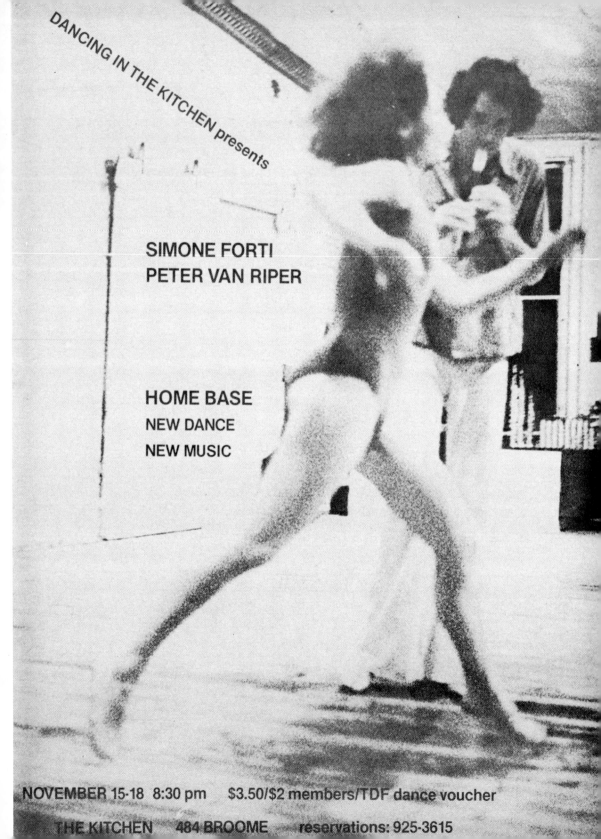

DANCING IN THE KITCHEN presents

SIMONE FORTI
PETER VAN RIPER

HOME BASE
NEW DANCE
NEW MUSIC

NOVEMBER 15-18   8:30 pm $3.50/$2 members/TDF dance voucher

THE KITCHEN   484 BROOME   reservations: 925-3615

HOME BASE

I once observed the pacing patterns of a female bear. She was the smaller of two, in an open enclosure with a little cave at the deep end. She was engaged in a kind of promenade, with certain paths which she would nearly always walk in the same sequence, stopping and turning at certain landmarks along the way. She would walk into the little cave and then back out swinging her head to clear the entrance and be on her way. Sometimes she would swing her head over, sometimes under. Then she would start out on her walk around the space, first along a rather narrow ledge at the end of which was a big rock nearly obstructing passage. The bear would usually stop there and turn around by swinging her head over or under, or occasionally by clearing the rock ass-side. At each stopping point she would make a choice between her various ways of turning. From time to time she would by-pass the big rock, gazing around as she paced out one of the less frequented loops in her pattern. It struck me that she had been able to regularize a matrix out of which she could improvise variations. I was especially interested to see whether the overhead and underhead turns determined with which foot forward she would begin the next lap of her course and so with which foot forward she would present herself to her next landmark. I tried to mirror her and to learn her dance by copying it as best I could from where I was. But she quickly became aware that I was dancing with her, and ending her practice came over to me as close as she could, stretching her long neck and sniffing in my direction.

''Home Base'' is one performance of an ongoing collaborative work in movement and sound. Peter Van Riper and I have been working together for nearly five years in this format which is partly improvisational, based on pre-established materials. This performance took place in November, 1979 at The Kitchen Center for Video, Music and Dance in New York. Each performance of this ongoing work has its own nature. In part, the character of the space where it is to take place determines what materials can flourish. We consider the acoustics, the floor, is it of stone or wood, how slippery is it. We select out of a large body of material, some that is old and some that is new. Above all, each performance is a unique point along the continuum as my dancing and Peter's music evolve, and comes to have its own character, its own face.

We usually begin a performance with an invocation in sound. Peter plays the molimo, or the moku gyo (a Japanese wooden bell), or the mbira (African thumb piano), some small instrument that sounds especially clear in the acoustics of the space. The molimo, a piece of flexible tubing usually used to connect household gas appliances, has acquired its musical life by chance. When blown through, it makes clear round tones, the harmonics break, rising and falling according to the air pressure. We call it the molimo after the horn pipe of the Pygmy, who used to make their instruments out of wood but now sometimes use a metal drain pipe. As Peter plays, he moves all through the space behind and in front of the audience. The audience listens, looks over the space in which the performance will take place, and watches the dancer sitting on the floor, listening.

Whenever possible we work in the semi-round. That is, we situate the audience along three sides of the performance area like a horseshoe. We like to have one clear wall as a resting place to move out from and return to.

All children dance. At a certain point, most people stop. Some go on to make it their main interest. As the musician works with sound and the sense of hearing, the dancer works with movement and the kinesthetic sense (''kinen,'' to move; ''aesthesis,'' to perceive). It is with this sense that we can tell without looking, whether our hand is still, opening or closing.

Some years ago, a few hours before having to perform, I was afraid that I had forgotten how to dance; I couldn't imagine dancing. I was standing outside the performance hall when, crouching slightly, I set my right foot forward and opened my hands to my sides. ''Is this how?'' I asked myself. I begin ''Day Night'' with this movement. Then a mysterious thing happens in my body. Of their own accord, my arms drift open in an upward curve. I continue with a series of phrases, each of which begins with that very particular gesture that I remember from years ago, and finishes with a movement from sleep. A certain familiar way of turning from my back to my side by reaching my right arm across my body until my spine is drawn around in a sequential whip like action. A certain way of turning from my side to my stomach and then to my other side. The music that Peter plays, ''Transverse Saxophone,'' grew out of collaborative work sessions, the influence back and forth between us being very intuitive, more a matter of sharing frame of mind rather than any particular structure or imagery. I simply worked on the movement that most recently interested me, while Peter worked on his new sound piece, a certain sequence of extended muted tones made by holding the saxophone quite horizontally. I place the phrases of movement here and there in the room, getting up at the end of each, looking around and deciding where to place the next, as simply as I would in my own studio. I set some familiar sleep movements or positions on end; I curl up on my side. I hold that position but tip it over so that I'm curled up

SIMONE FORTI & PETER VAN RIPER

HOME BASE

molimo invocation

day night / transverse saxophone

zoo mantras

circling / circle song - broken

six / double sound - broken

doppler

intermission

garden / garden

twig

sleep walk / double depth

turning in place / moku gyo

HOME BASE is in the format which we have been using in all our work in our traveling. Always the performance is composed of various materials, some dating back several years, some just emerging, and is tailored to each situation in consideration of the space, the floor, the acoustics, the place, the time. New York is our home base.

facing downwards, balanced on my elbows and knees. Then I set that same position up on end, onto my feet, still curled up as in sleep. Interposed between two such phrases is one of a different nature from a different origin. On the wall at my desk there are two post cards. One is of a statuette of the Egyptian god Horus I once saw at the Louvre, poised in a striding stance, hands held forward at shoulder height, very like a vessel of offering or receiving. The other card, sent to me by a dancer friend, Pooh Kaye, is of an anonymous youth leaping across a chasm. I take a running start, jump as far as I can. As I land I turn to face the direction from which I came and pause in the posture of Horus, my hands in place as if to catch the jumper. My arms drift open and out and I think of the moment of passing between walking and sleeping.

"Zoo Mantras" is a solo which dates back to a time before I started working with music, when I first started developing material from observations of animals in the zoo.

Brown bear walk: front limb steps and whole side contracts to pull back limb into place. Boom boo-boom. Boom boo-boom. Boom boo-boom. Giraffe: back limb steps, crowds forelimb which steps ahead. Boom boom. Boom boom.

I observed the structure of animals' movements, I also observed what seemed to me a kind of dance behavior.

I saw an elephant who had perfected a walk with which he passed the time of day. It was a walking backwards and forwards, some four to seven steps each way with, at either end, a slight kick which served to absorb the momentum and to reverse the direction of travel of that great and finely-balanced bulk.

"Zoo Mantras" consists of four blocks of movement. The first is derived from the elephant walk. I try to keep my steps as smooth as the elephant's and with that same lilting rocking in my spine. Sometimes, instead of the slight kick, there is an instant when I poise my toes on the ground, ankle relaxed. I continue, absorbed in this subtle movement game, until I suddenly realize that I've been doing this for quite some time, for long enough, and simply walk away to the place of the next beginning. Hopefully the audience too has been absorbed, for I believe that we see a movement not only with our eyes, but identify with it through our kinesthetic sense as well. My next movement is a roll on the ground. I imagine that I am being rolled across the room by the rising of the ocean tide and then back again by the ocean tide's receding. I'm very conscious of the force of gravity, and of how smoothly the body, consisting in great part of water, can roll along.

On a tiny island of cement, made to look like an ice-flow, the polar bear spends hours swinging his head.

Taking the stance of the polar bear, I swing my head in an arc, and swing and swing and swing and swing and swing. I recently gained a great deal more insight into this movement from a film by another dancer friend, Yoshiko Chuma. In her closing sequence she swings the weight of her head from side to side. Because she is on a platform floating on a lake, her swinging sets her platform to rocking. She ends by dropping into the water.

Often movements have a natural aging process, like any idea. At first they are new, a little rough, it's fun to work on them, to try to resolve them. Then they become full and eloquent. It sometimes happens that they start to feel a bit calcified, a bit confused and empty.

"Circling" grew out of studies to sense momentum in the forward striding walk. Invariably, I would reach the end of the available space. I found that if I leaned my weight to one side, my walk would immediately follow a curve in that direction. It's the same with riding a bicycle. Anyone who has enjoyed making serpentine curves or figure eights on a bicycle can well understand how I came to spend so much time striding along, tipping my weight into curves to the left and to the right. I played with the fine points of balance, using my arms as levers, shifting my spine, the weight of my head. These movements were reflected in the floor patterns through which I was propelled. I found that I could stride along in a small circle, leaning my weight heavily into the center, supported by the centrifugal force. "Circle Song" consists of fast repetitive sets of high frequencies evolving in circular progression on Eb sopranino saxophone. My striding, circling, and slaloming sometimes rides in time with the shimmering tones, more often not, as our phrasings merge and diverge. I evolved many mandala-like patterns. After a time the patterns became imprinted in my memory, and as that happened I seemed to lose the ability to simply play with those fine points of balance. It came to me that I should hold two small bowls of rice as I circled. My movement was new again. The image was different. To keep the rice from flying from the bowls I had to take the curves with a new simplicity and clarity.

"Six" is closely related to "Circling." It is a dynamic study of the figures zero through nine of the Arabic numerals, which are contained within a geometric plan of seven circles and two intersecting triangles. The zero is the elipse which encompasses the two circles which form the figure eight; the figure one passes straight down the center, etc. In a sense I use the numerals as a floor pattern, but I try to move through the curves and straight lines as dynamically as possible. In that way my sense of the figures is really kinesthetic; I work with the centrifugal and other forces with a sense of measure. The reach of my arm gives me my initial radius which I then expand. I usually call this study "Zero" and trace the figures zero through nine. But in the context of "Home Base" I felt that tracing the numbers up to six was the right measure. Peter plays "Double Sound," a piece with continuous repetitive sound, closely related to "Circle Song," this one on Bb soprano saxophone.

One side of Peter's record album "Sound To Movement," is a recording of a live performance in the Museum of Modern Art, Oxford, England. The room had such a resonant floor that my footfalls can be heard in counter-point with Peter's playing. My dancing and Peter's music go through stages of developing separately and together. We work with materials until we arrive at a certain point of definition, but try to time ourselves so that the crest of the wave of realizing the piece comes at the time of performance. It's Peter's nature to accept a plan emerging relatively early in the preparations, as a stable point of reference, as a commitment. I always feel that a plan is tentative, and often want to make some basic changes almost at the last minute, changing the order of the sections, bringing in something else, leaving something out. Our two ways are like the hammer and fire out of which we shape our work.

"Doppler" is a solo for soprano and sopranino saxophones. With the first instrument Peter introduces a simple series of tones. Then, picking up the soprano, he restates the tones in this lower voice and gradually begins to spin in place as he plays, holding the tones long so that you can hear them rise and fall as the horn swings by, creating a doppler effect like a passing train whistle.

"Garden" is a landscape. I place a stone here, I place a stone there, here a bush, there I jump this way; that way, taller bushes. I slide along the length of the space, a stream. A frog jumps. Peter plays natural bird tones on recorder, a small ocarina, and two bamboo sticks which he hits together. They make a sound like we once heard storks make with their beaks after a rain storm. It's not so much that I make myself look like a stone. It's more that, in placing myself, I become something that has the presence of a stone. A rock here, over there a rock and, by it, another and another, a rock there, and over there, and next to it others next to others, and a rock over there and there and there, that one among those and down over there those others and this one and this rock and this one here.

"Twig," my new solo, grew out of observations of gorillas playing, The game seemed to consist of shifting the weight around, reaching out an arm or a leg in one form of support and then another, making one change of position after another in a smooth ongoing succession of shifts of weight. As the gorillas had been playing on a multi-leveled ground, I used a sturdy low table to give me something to climb up and down from. And I had a twig or light stick which I carried in my curled fingers, in my toes, I picked it up with my lips, I hung from the twig, or seemed to, I held it firmly in my teeth and twanged it with my finger as I had once seen a chimp do, creating a wonderful sound in my head. "Twig" was the most clearly representational piece of the evening. I ended it in quite human posture, seated at the work bench, stick in hand, like a writing instrument, and as I drew my arm from left to right, the stick traced a wide arc on the flat surface before me.

"Sleep Walk" and "Double Depth" are very closely knitted in movement and sound, to me, very much a unified event. In this section Peter plays soprano saxophone along with a recorded tape. The tape is of "Circle Song," but it is played back at a slow speed, thus acquiring the underwater quality that suggested its name. The live playing takes its cue from this slower and lower sound and interfaces with it. The movement begins with what I call a crescent roll, a slow roll across the space, body kept in a constant crescent curve while turning on itself, like the edge of a smoke ring. Then I rise and establish a landscape of verticals, stepping over here, then over there, placing an upward extended position in each spot. As Peter plays he wanders through the space. Then I lie down and begin an ongoing succession of turns and moves as one makes in sleep. One of these, a turn from the back to the side, entails a whip-like action in the spine. I've discovered that if I isolate that spine action and repeat it many times as I lie on my side, it propels me along the floor. I whip my way along sometimes following the sounds of the live horn, sometimes those of the recorded past beneath it, back up the path I earlier established as a stream in "Garden". I rise, and running in a small circle, heavily rest my weight towards its center, on the centrifugal force. Curving out of the circle, leaning this way and that,

Grizley

Turning corner

Turning ramp

I bank in a serpentine path until suddenly I confront the demon. In the midst of my riding the smooth curves my wrist is seized in the teeth of an imaginary dog. In an instant I dislodge my arm, swat the dog twice on the head, as hard as I can, throw up my arms and go running backwards nearly out of control. Then, as if nothing had happened, some more verticals, and I place myself on the low table, in the position of a hippopotamus half reclining on its side, like an Egyptian statuette of some two thousand years past, of Ta-Weret, protector of women, and listen to the last phrases that Peter, walking through the space filled with sound, is playing.

"Turning in Place" with "Moku Gyo," as the last section, has a function akin to the invocation. It is a closing and it is simple. Moku gyo means wooden fish in Japanese. It is a Buddhist wooden bell. As Peter walks around striking the wood bell whose sound is mellow and precise and slightly different from place to place, according to the acoustics of the room, I stand in the very center, doing a simple swinging of arms and legs which makes me turn in place, a quarter turn at the time, and for the first time in the performance I look squarely into the faces in the audience, a kind of greeting. The audience is on three sides of us, but I don't neglect to also face and greet the fourth and empty side.

("Home Base" was first published in CONTACT QUARTERLY, Vol. V, No. 3/4 Spring/Summer 1980 and is an addition to the second printing.)

Acknowledgements

Acknowledgement is due to the following for photographs, documents and other matter reprinted in this book. Uncited drawings and diagrams by Simone Forti.

1 — Photograph by Simone Forti.

9 — "Onion Walk," first printed in *An Anthology,* edited by La Monte Young and Jackson MacLow, New York, 1963.

30 — Ann Halprin's summer workshop, 1959. *[standing, clockwise from bottom left]* Trisha Brown, Shirley Ririe, June Ekman, Sunny Bloland, A. H., Lisa Strauss, Paul Pera, Willis Ward; *[seated on steps from top to bottom]* Yvonne Rainer, Ruth Emerson, S. F., Jerrie Glover, A.A. Leath, unknown, unknown, John Graham. Photographer unknown.

37-38 — Reuben Gallery announcement, 1960.

40, 41, 43 — First performance of "See-Saw," Reuben Gallery, New York, 1960. Photographs by Robert R. McElroy.

45-46 — First performance of "Rollers," Reuben Gallery, 1960. Photographs by Robert R. McElroy.

47-55 — Pages from Simone Forti's 1961 New York journal.

57 — "Slantboard," Pasadena Museum of Art, 1971. Photograph by Serge Tcherepnin.

58 — "Huddle," Loeb Student Center, New York University, 1969. Photograph by Peter Moore.

60 — Floor plan of 1961 concert on Chambers Street, New York, drawn by Simone Forti.

63 — "Platforms," Loeb Student Center, New York University, 1961. Photograph by Peter Moore.

65 — "Accompaniment for La Monte's 2 sounds and La Monte's 2 sounds," Cornell School of Architecture, New York, 1969. Photograph by Peter Moore.

71 — Score for "Elevation Tune No. 2," 1967.

72-77 — Score for "Face Tunes," 1967.

77 — Some members of the audience during a performance of "Face Tunes" at the Cornell School of Architecture, New York, 1969. Photograph by Peter Moore.

80 — Still from a 16mm film of "Cloths," 1967. Camera: Hollis Frampton.

82-83 — Images projected during a performance of "Book." Photographs by Simone Forti.

84 — Image projected during a performance of "Bottom." Photograph by Florence J. Beckers, Rushmore Foto.

87-88 — Original performance of "Fallers," Cornell School of Architecture, New York, 1967. Photographs by Peter More.

90 — "Sleepwalkers," Loeb Student Center, New York University, 1969. Photograph by Peter Moore.

95-98 — Pages from Simone Forti's Italy journal, 1968-69.

103 — This Hopi tradition is discussed at length in *The Book of the Hopi* by Frank Waters, Viking Press, New York, 1963.

110-112 — Pages from Simone Forti's 1971 California journal.

118-120 — Fragments from an early draft of *Handbook in Motion.*

128 — Work session at Musee Galliera, Paris, 1973. Photograph by Christophe Kuhn.

130 — An evening of music and dance, Grand Union Dance Gallery, New York, 1973. Photograph by Peter Moore.

138 — Work session, California Institute of the Arts, 1973. Photograph by Alvin Comiter.

140 — Work session, Grand Union Dance Gallery, New York. Photograph by Peter Moore.

142 — Poster design by Peter Van Riper with photo by Merel Steir, 1979.